What people are saying

"Here at Citibank we use the Quick Course® computer training book series for 'just-in-time' job aids—the books are great for users who are too busy for tutorials and training. Quick Course® books provide very clear instruction and easy reference."

Bill Moreno, Development Manager
Citibank
San Francisco, CA

"At Geometric Results, much of our work is PC related and we need training tools that can quickly and effectively improve the PC skills of our people. Early this year we began using your materials in our internal PC training curriculum and the results have been outstanding. Both participants and instructors like the books and the measured learning outcomes have been very favorable."

Roger Hill, Instructional Systems Designer
Geometric Results Incorporated
Southfield, MI

"The concise and well organized text features numbered instructions, screen shots, and useful quick reference pointers, and tips…[This] affordable text is very helpful for educators who wish to build proficiency."

Computer Literacy column
Curriculum Administrator Magazine
Stamford, CT

"I have purchased five other books on this subject that I've probably paid more than \$60 for, and your [Quick Course®] book taught me more than those five books combined!"

Emory Majors
Searcy, AR

"I would like you to know how much I enjoy the Quick Course® books I have received from you. The directions are clear and easy to follow with attention paid to every detail of the particular lesson."

Betty Weinkauf, Retired Senior
Mission, TX

QUICK COURSE®

in

MICROSOFT®

WINDOWS

95

ONLINE PRESS INC.

Microsoft Press

PUBLISHED BY
Microsoft Press
A Division of Microsoft Corporation
One Microsoft Way
Redmond, WA 98052-6399

Library of Congress Cataloging-in-Publication Data

Quick Course in Microsoft Windows 95 / Online Press Inc.
    p.   cm.
  Includes index.
  ISBN 1-57231-727-2
  1. Microsoft Windows (Computer file)   2. Operating systems
(Computers)   I. Online Press Inc.
QA76.76.O63Q52   1997
005.469--dc21   97-27388
                                                        CIP

Printed and bound in the United States of America.

2 3 4 5 6 7 8 9 WCWC 2 1 0 9 8

Distributed to the book trade in Canada by Macmillan of Canada, a division of Canada Publishing Corporation.

A CIP record of this book is available from the British Library.

Microsoft Press books are available through booksellers and distributors worldwide. For further information about international editions, contact your local Microsoft Corporation office. Or contact Microsoft Press International directly at fax (425) 936-7329.

A Quick Course® Education/Training Edition for this title is published by Online Press Inc. For information about supplementary workbooks, contact Online Press Inc. at 14320 NE 21st St., Suite 18, Bellevue, WA, 98007, USA, 1-800-854-3344.

Authors: Joyce Cox of Online Press Inc., Bellevue, Washington
Acquisitions Editor: Susanne M. Freet
Project Editor: Maureen Williams Zimmerman

From the publisher

"I love these books!"

I can't tell you the number of times people have said those exact words to me about our new Quick Course® software training book series. And when I ask them what makes the books so special, this is what they say:

- **They're short and approachable, but they give you hours worth of good information.**

  Written for busy people with limited time, most Quick Course books are designed to be completed in 15 to 40 hours. Because Quick Course books are usually divided into two parts—Learning the Basics and Building Proficiency—users can selectively choose the chapters that meet their needs and complete them as time allows.

- **They're relevant and fun, and they assume you're no dummy.**

  Written in an easy-to-follow, step-by-step format, Quick Course books offer streamlined instruction for the new user in the form of no-nonsense, to-the-point tutorials and learning exercises. Each book provides a logical sequence of instructions for creating useful business documents—the same documents people use on the job. People can either follow along directly or substitute their own information and customize the documents. After finishing a book, users have a valuable "library" of documents they can continually recycle and update with new information.

- **They're direct and to the point, and they're a lot more than just pretty pictures.**

  Training-oriented rather than feature-oriented, Quick Course books don't cover the things you don't really need to know to do useful work. They offer easy-to-follow, step-by-step instructions; lots of screen shots for checking work in progress; quick-reference pointers for fast, easy lookup and review; and useful tips offering additional information on topics being discussed.

- **They're a rolled-into-one-book solution, and they meet a variety of training needs.**

  Designed with instructional flexibility in mind, Quick Course books can be used both for self-training and as the basis for weeklong courses, two-day seminars, and all-day workshops. They can be adapted to meet a variety of training needs, including classroom instruction, take-away practice exercises, and self-paced learning.

Microsoft Press is very excited about bringing you this extraordinary series. But you must be the judge. I hope you'll give these books a try. And maybe the next time I see you, you too will say, "Hey, Jim! I love these books!"

Jim Brown, Publisher
Microsoft Press

Content overview

Content details

3 Increasing Your Efficiency   56

4 Solving Common Problems   90

1

Introducing Windows 95

While using WordPad to create a document, we demonstrate how to start programs, work with windows, and choose commands using menus and toolbar buttons. We also show you how to get help and then how to shut down the computer.

Choose commands from menus
or use toolbar buttons

Manipulate all program,
folders, and document
windows the same way

Use buttons to expand
and contract windows
and close programs

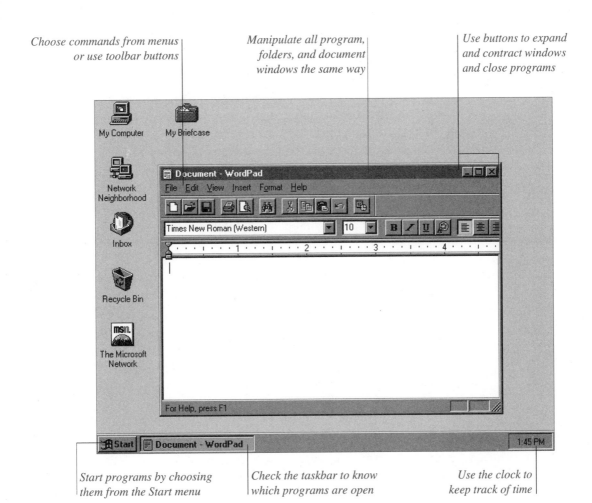

Start programs by choosing
them from the Start menu

Check the taskbar to know
which programs are open

Use the clock to
keep track of time

W indows 95, Microsoft's new operating system, replaces MS-DOS or PC-DOS (Microsoft Disk Operating System or PC Disk Operating System, both called DOS from now on) and Windows 3.*x* to create a new way of working with your computer. (Windows 3.*x* is shorthand for all the versions belonging to the third generation of Windows: Windows 3.0, 3.1, and 3.11, and Windows for Workgroups 3.1 and 3.11.) Whereas earlier versions of Windows created a "graphical environment" on top of DOS and used DOS to perform basic computer operations, Windows 95 shoulders the responsibility for all operating system tasks in addition to providing a set of tools that give you a visual way of telling the computer what you want to do.

Many people were persuaded to start using PCs because Windows 3.*x* was supposed to make computing easy. They liked the fact that they no longer had to type obscure commands to get their work done. They simply clicked a picture called an *icon* or selected a command from a list called a *menu* to tell Windows what they wanted it to do. Nevertheless, there were constant complaints that though Windows made using PCs easier, the program was not intuitive enough. Windows 95 addresses this complaint by completely revamping the look and feel of Windows while enhancing the features that made Windows 3.*x* so popular, such as multitasking (running two or more programs concurrently), which saves time by allowing you to keep all the information you need at your fingertips, and easy transfer of information from one program to another.

In this book, we take a tour of Windows 95, covering all the features most people need to know to get their daily work done. We assume that Windows 95 is installed on your computer, the computer is turned on, and you are ready to go. So without any more preamble, let's get started.

The Desktop

When you turn on your computer, Windows 95 rushes around setting everything up, and when it's finished, you see a screen that looks something like this one:

Switching from Windows or Windows for Workgroups?

You might think that knowing Windows or Windows for Workgroups 3.*x* will give you a jump start on getting down to work with Windows 95, but studies have shown that totally novice computer users often learn basic Windows 95 techniques faster than former Windows or Windows for Workgroups users. Why? Because they don't spend time looking for the equivalents of old Windows components such as Program Manager, File Manager, and Task Manager. They focus on what they want to do and how they can do it with Windows 95, instead of adding the step of constantly translating to and from old Windows. If you are an old Windows hand, you may find it faster to come up to speed with the new operating system if you approach the learning of Windows 95 with an open mind and if, at least initially, you resist the temptation to compare the new program with the old.

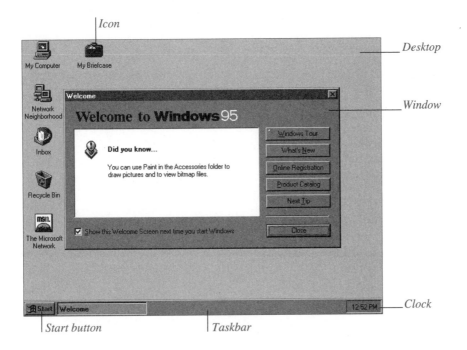

The Windows opening screen is known as the *desktop*. This well-worn metaphor is designed to make using the tools available with Windows no more intimidating than using the familiar tools found on a typical desk in a typical office. On the desktop shown above is a window that displays a welcome message and a tip. Also visible are six icons that represent different Windows tools, and a taskbar with a Start button at

Networked computers

When you turn on a computer that is connected to a network, you see a box in which you must enter your name and password in order to log onto the network. (Windows 95 may enter the name for you.) Once this step is complete, you see the desktop.

Shared computers

If Windows 95 has been set up on your computer with a "user profile" for each person who uses the computer, you see a box in which you must enter your name and password whenever you turn on the computer. Windows then sets up the computer according to your profile. You can find out more about user profiles by double-clicking the Passwords icon in Control Panel and clicking the User Profiles tab (see page 131).

Program window instead of desktop?

If you turn on your computer and wind up with a program already started, that program has been added to the StartUp group on the Programs submenu of the Start menu. (See page 66 for more information.) You can simply click the Close button (the button with an X) at the right end of the title bar to close the program and display the desktop.

one end and a notification area and a clock at the other. (The notification area tells you the status of various components of your system, such as your printer or modem.) The icons and taskbar are the primary tools you'll use to get your Windows work done, and you'll learn all about them in this book.

The pointer

Floating somewhere on the desktop is the *pointer*, which is electronically connected to your mouse. The mouse is essential equipment for working with Windows and Windows programs, also known as *applications*. As you move the mouse, the pointer moves correspondingly on the screen, allowing you to point to the item you want to work with. The pointer is often an arrow, but it can take other forms, such as an I-beam when over text or an hourglass when Windows is processing information. When the pointer is where you want it, you click one of the mouse buttons to activate the item under it, choose commands, and so on, or you double-click to give other types of instructions.

Using the mouse

Clicking is simply a matter of pressing and releasing the mouse button once. *Double-clicking* works the same way, except that you quickly click the mouse button twice. In this book, we assume that you are using the left mouse button as your primary button and your right mouse button as your secondary button. So when we say *Click the Recycle Bin*, we

No taskbar?

If the taskbar is nowhere in sight, you can display it by holding down the Ctrl key while you press the Esc key. (This action is known as *pressing Ctrl+Esc*.) If the taskbar is not at the bottom of your screen but instead rests against one of the other three edges, you can leave it where it is and still follow along with our examples. Or you can move it by pointing to it, holding down the mouse button, dragging to the bottom of the screen, and releasing the mouse button (see page 133).

Displaying the date

If you want to check the date, point to the clock at the right end of the taskbar. A box containing the current date pops up. See page 120 for information about how to adjust the date and time and change the way they are displayed.

mean *Move the pointer over the Recycle Bin and click the left mouse button*. If you have reversed the primary and secondary buttons, you would click the right mouse button instead. Similarly, when we say *Right-click the clock*, we mean *Move the pointer to the clock and click the right mouse button*. If you have reversed the buttons, you would click the left mouse button instead. (We describe how to reverse the buttons on page 126.)

Let's start by dealing with the Welcome window. (If you don't ◄— see a Welcome window on your screen, read the following paragraphs but skip the instructions.) You will do almost all of your work with Windows in some sort of window (a rectangle with a title bar across the top that describes the function of the window or shows the name of the document and program displayed in it). In this case, the window displays some tidbit of information about Windows 95. If you want, you can click Windows Tour to take a brief tour of Windows 95 or click What's New to get an overview of improvements in the program. You can also click Online Registration to send registration information over your modem to Microsoft or click Next Tip to see a different tip. (You might also see a Product Catalog button, which you can click to get information about other Microsoft and Windows 95 products.)

The Welcome window

At the right end of the Welcome window's title bar is a *Close button* designated with an X. You can either click this button or click the Close button in the bottom right corner of the window to close the Welcome window. Follow these steps:

1. Move the mouse so that the pointer is over the check box in the bottom left corner of the Welcome window and click the box to remove the check mark, which deselects the option. That way, you won't see this window every time you turn on your computer.

2. Click the Close button at the right end of the title bar to close ◄— the window.

The Close button

We'll talk more about check boxes and buttons later in this chapter. For now, let's explore.

Starting Programs

If you are like most computer users, you aren't interested in computers and their programs for their own sakes. You want to do useful work. You want to send a letter, jot down notes for a meeting, draft a report, or analyze your income and expenses for the month. So the first thing you want to know about Windows is how do you start a program and create and save a document.

The simplest way to get going is to start a program from the *Start menu*, which is displayed when you click the *Start button* at the left end of the taskbar. (Some people use the terms *running*, *executing*, *launching*, and *loading* to mean *starting* a program. Generally, these terms can be used interchangeably.) Try this:

The Start button

1. Move the pointer to the Start button at the left end of the taskbar at the bottom of the screen. A small box with the words *Click here to begin* appears.

2. Click the Start button to display this Start menu:

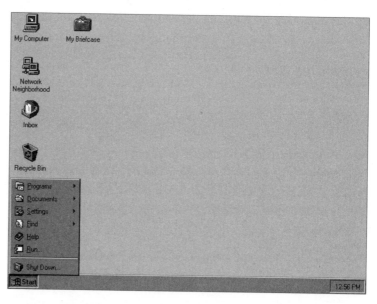

Menus

A menu is simply a list of *commands* you can choose to tell Windows to carry out specific tasks. In this case, the commands are for basic tasks such as starting programs, finding and loading documents, changing system settings, and getting information.

3. Move the pointer to Programs but don't click. Windows displays a *submenu* of programs preceded by unique icons and program groups preceded by folder icons. Clicking a program name starts that program and moving the pointer to a program group displays yet another submenu.

Submenus

4. Move the pointer onto the submenu and then to Accessories, but again, don't click. Windows lists all the programs that are part of the Accessories program group, and your screen now looks like this:

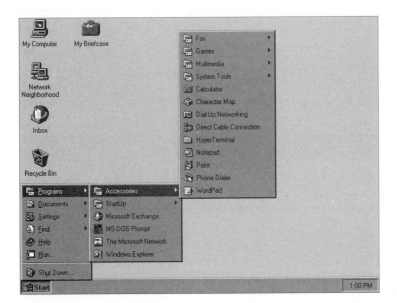

Start menu variations

Your Start menu may look different from the one we show, depending on what programs are installed on your computer and whether your Start menu has been customized. See page 63 for information about how to add items to the Start menu.

Program Manager groups

When you upgrade to Windows 95 from Windows or Windows for Workgroups 3.*x*, Windows 95 includes your Program Manager groups on the Programs submenu of the Start menu. You can change these groups in Windows 95 by customizing the Start menu (see page 63).

Starting WordPad → 5. Move the pointer onto the third menu and down to WordPad, and click to start the WordPad program, a simple word processor that comes with Windows 95. When WordPad is loaded, you see this window on your screen:

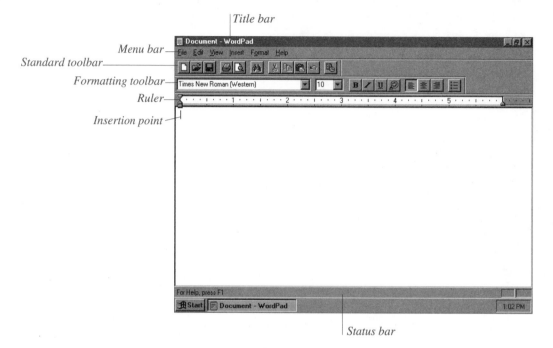

Notice that a button representing the WordPad window has appeared on the taskbar to the right of the Start button. We'll talk more about this button in a moment.

Window Basics

As we've said, when you're working with Windows 95 or with a Windows-based program, you're always working in a window, so it makes sense to learn some basic windowing skills before we go any further.

Window Anatomy

The window now on your screen has many of the characteristics of windows used by Windows 95 programs. At the top is the title bar, which tells you that the window contains an untitled, currently blank, WordPad document. (A *docu-*

A full taskbar

If you open many windows, the taskbar can get pretty full of buttons. Windows then abbreviates the button names in order to accommodate them all. If you can't tell which window a button represents, point to the button for a brief moment, and the full window name will pop up.

ment is a file you create.) Below the title bar is a *menu bar*, which lists the command menus available for WordPad. Below the menu bar are two *toolbars*, collections of buttons that you can click to quickly carry out often-used commands. (We'll talk more about the various ways of giving commands in a moment.) Below them is a *ruler*, a handy measuring tool that helps you design more complicated documents. At the bottom of this window is a *status bar*, where the program posts various items of useful information. Occupying the majority of the window is the *work area*, where you create the document. In this area, a blinking *insertion point* indicates where the next character you type will appear. (Don't confuse the insertion point with the pointer, which moves with your mouse and doesn't blink.)

Back to the title bar. At the left end is the Control-menu icon. Clicking this icon displays a menu of commands for sizing and moving the window and quitting the program. (You can carry out these commands in other, simpler ways, so we won't cover this menu in detail here.) At the right end of the title bar is the same Close button you used to close the Welcome window, and next to the Close button are two buttons that we need to examine a little closer.

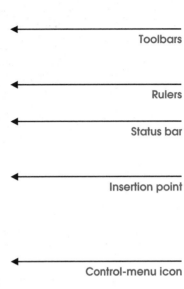

Toolbars

Rulers

Status bar

Insertion point

Control-menu icon

Sizing and Moving Windows

With many programs, you will want to work in a window that occupies the entire screen so that you can see as much of each document as possible. Sometimes, however, you will want the window to take up less of the screen so that you can see other items on your desktop. Windows puts two buttons at the right end of the title bar of many windows so that you can quickly contract and expand the windows. You can also size the windows manually. Try this:

1. Point to the *Restore button* (the middle of the three buttons on the title bar) and click. The Wordpad window contracts to about half-size and the *Maximize button* replaces the Restore button on the title bar, as shown on the next page.

The Restore button

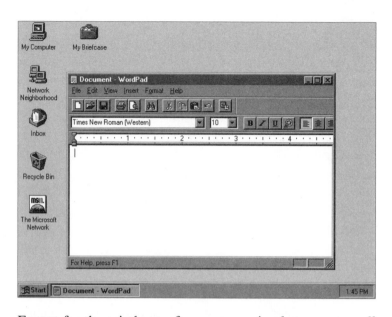

Window frames

Except for the windows of some very simple programs, all windows that don't occupy the entire screen have *frames*, and most frames can stretch and shrink to make their windows larger or smaller. As you move the pointer over different parts of a frame that is resizable, the pointer becomes a double-headed arrow, indicating the directions in which you can drag the frame to change its size. You can drag the sides of the window frame to the left and right, drag the top and bottom of the frame up and down, and drag the corners up and down diagonally.

2. Point to the left side of the window's frame and when the pointer changes to a double-headed arrow, hold down the left mouse button, move the mouse to the left to make the window wider, and release the mouse button. This action is called *dragging*.

3. Point to the bottom of the frame and drag up until the window is about 2 inches tall.

4. Point to the window's title bar and drag to the right. A shadow image of the window's frame indicates how far the window will move, and when you release the mouse button, the window snaps into place.

Program windows vs. document windows

Some application programs, such as word processors and spreadsheets, let you have more than one document open at the same time. These programs open each document in a separate window that is contained within the program window. Document windows can be sized and moved, but only within the frame of the program window.

The Maximize button

5. Now click the Maximize button on the title bar to expand the window so that it fills the screen. The Maximize button is replaced by the Restore button, and the window's frame disappears. (Because a maximized window doesn't have a frame, you can't manually resize it.)

6. Click the Restore button again. The window contracts to its previous size.

Restoring windows to their previous size

The *Minimize button* (the left of the three buttons on the title bar) shrinks the window to its minimum size and hides it under its button on the taskbar. The window still contains your document and the program you are using to create it, but the window is inactive and tucked out of sight, as you'll see if you follow these steps:

The Minimize button

1. Click the Minimize button on the title bar. The window appears to shrink into its button on the taskbar, and the button turns gray to indicate that its window is no longer active.

2. Redisplay the window by clicking the button labeled *Document - WordPad* on the taskbar.

3. Finally, click the Maximize button to expand the window to fill the screen.

Command Basics

To get any useful work done in Windows, you have to be able to tell the computer what to do. Windows provides a number of methods for giving instructions. We'll look at the primary methods in this section.

Choosing Commands from Menus

You've already gotten a taste of how to choose commands from the Start menu to start a program. Here we'll look at a couple of other kinds of menus.

Using Menu-Bar Menus

In most Windows programs, you usually carry out tasks by choosing commands from the menus listed on the menu bar at the top of the program's window. In the menu bar, you click

Flipping between Restore and Maximize

When a window is maximized, you can also restore it to its previous size by double-clicking its title bar. Double-clicking the title bar of a restored window maximizes the window.

the name of the menu you want, and the menu drops down, displaying its list of commands. As part of the effort to give all Windows programs a common look, menus with commands that carry out similar tasks often have the same names in different programs. The File menu and Help menu are examples of common menus. For instance, the File menu usually contains commands such as New (for creating new windows or documents), Open (for opening documents), Save (for saving the current document), and Exit (to leave the program).

To choose a command from a menu, you simply click the command. To close a menu without choosing a command, you either click an empty spot away from the menu or press the Esc key. Let's take a look at a few menus and choose a command or two:

Displaying menu-bar menus

1. Click the word *Edit* on the menu bar to drop down the Edit menu shown here:

Choosing commands with the keyboard

If you find it faster to use the keyboard, you can activate the menu bar by pressing Alt and then open the menu by typing the underlined letter in the menu name. Next choose a command by typing the underlined letter in the command name. Once you learn the letters for menus and commands, you can type the key sequence quickly to choose the command. For example, to quit many programs, you can press Alt, then F, and then X.

All Windows programs present their menu commands in consistent ways and use these visual cues to tell you various things about the commands:

- Commands that perform related tasks are grouped, and the group is separated from other commands by a line.

- Some commands are displayed in "gray" letters, indicating they are not currently available. For example, most programs have Cut and Copy commands on their Edit menus, and these commands appear in gray letters until your document contains information that can be cut or copied.

- Some commands are followed by an ellipsis (...), indicating that you must supply more information in a special kind of window called a dialog box before the command can be carried out. (More about dialog boxes in a moment.)

  Commands with ellipses

- Key combinations are listed to the right of some commands, indicating that you can bypass the menu and carry out the command by pressing the corresponding keyboard shortcut.

  Commands with key combinations

- Some command names are followed by a triangle, indicating that the command has a submenu. (You saw how to choose commands from a submenu when you started WordPad from the Start menu.)

  Commands with triangles

- Some commands are preceded by a check mark, indicating that you can "toggle" the command on and off.

  Commands with check marks

  The commands on the Edit menu illustrate the first four visual cues in this list.

2. Now move the pointer over the word *View* on the menu bar to drop down that menu. (Notice that once one menu is open, you don't have to click to open another.)

3. Move the pointer down to the Ruler command and click. WordPad turns off the command and removes the ruler from the window.

   Choosing commands with the mouse

4. Click View on the menu bar to display the View menu again, notice that the Ruler command is no longer preceded by a check mark, and then click Ruler to turn on the command and redisplay the ruler.

Dialog Boxes

Dialog boxes are Windows' way of allowing you to give information or to select from several different options so that a particular command can be carried out exactly the way you want it. To demonstrate, let's create a memo:

1. Type *MEMO* and press Enter twice.

2. Type *To: All Staff*, press Enter, type *From: Julia*, press Enter, and then type *Date:* and a space.

Correcting mistakes

If you make a mistake while typing the memo, the simplest way to correct it is to press the Backspace key until you've erased the error and then retype the text correctly. If you want to move the insertion point to correct an error, point to the place in the existing text where you want the insertion point to appear and then click the left mouse button. Or you can use the Arrow keys to move the insertion point anywhere in the existing text.

3. To insert the date, choose the Date And Time command from the Insert menu by clicking Insert on the menu bar to display that menu's list of commands (in this case, the objects that can be inserted in a WordPad document) and then clicking Date And Time. WordPad checks your computer for the current date and time and then displays the date and time in various formats in this dialog box:

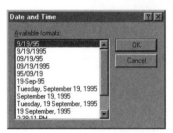

Using the scroll bars

When windows are not big enough to display all of their contents, Windows provides vertical and horizontal scroll bars so that you can bring other parts of the window's contents into view. You use the vertical scroll bar to move the contents up and down and the horizontal scroll bar to move the contents from side to side. Manipulating scroll bars is an important way of getting around in Windows. You can use a couple of different scrolling methods. Clicking the arrow at either end of a scroll bar moves the contents a line or a column at a time, whereas clicking on either side of the scroll box on the scroll bar moves the contents a "windowful" at a time. The position of the scroll box in relation to the scroll bar tells you where you are in the contents. For example, when the scroll box is in the middle of the scroll bar, the window is positioned roughly halfway through its contents. The size of the scroll box tells you about how much of the contents you can see at one time. For example, if the scroll box is half the length of the scroll bar, you can see half the contents.

This dialog box is very simple and presents only one set of options, but as you'll see, dialog boxes can be pretty complex, with options arranged in layered categories called *tabs*. (An example of a tabbed dialog box is shown on page 23.) Here, you indicate the format you want for the date by selecting the format from a *list box*. The list of possible formats is too long to fit in its box, so a *scroll bar* appears down the right side, allowing you to scroll the list up and down to bring out-of-sight options into view. (See the adjacent tip for more information about scroll bars.)

4. Click the arrowhead, called a *scroll arrow*, at the bottom of the scroll bar on the right side of the list box to see the other available date and time options.

5. Click the format that is the equivalent of *August 24, 1995* to select it. Windows indicates your selection by changing it to white type on a dark background.

6. Click OK. WordPad inserts the current date in the selected format in the memo.

7. Press Enter, type *Subject: Directions to staff party*, press Enter three times, type the following note, and press Enter where indicated:

As promised, here are directions to the Deer Creek Country Club. See you all there on February 14!

(Press Enter twice)

1. Take I-5 North to Alderfield.
2. Take Exit 217 and turn right onto Deer Creek Road.
3. Follow the road up-hill and down-dale for 7 miles, until you see Tiny's Trading Post on your left.
4. Turn right onto Salish Road, and the entrance to Deer Creek Country Club is immediately on the left by the statue of grazing deer.

(Press Enter)

Here are the results:

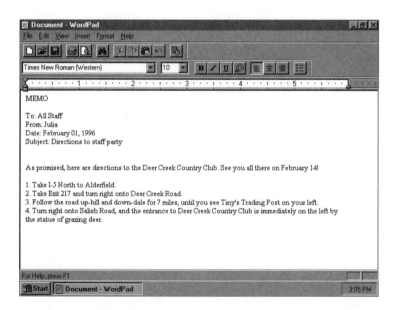

Now let's save the document. In the process, you'll use a more complex dialog box to specify a filename for the document, specify where to store it, and create a folder to hold this and related documents. You'll also get an idea of how your computer's storage (the electronic equivalent of your filing cabinet) is structured.

1. Choose the Save As command from the File menu. WordPad displays the Save As dialog box shown on the next page.

Saving WordPad documents

All Windows dialog boxes request information in consistent ways and like commands, use visual cues to let you know the kind of information they need and how you should give it. The most common dialog box components are:

Edit boxes

- You enter variable information, such as filenames, by typing it in an *edit box*, represented in the Save As dialog box by the File Name box. If you want to replace an existing entry in an edit box, simply select the entry and overtype the old text with the new. You can double-click the edit box to select the entry quickly.

List boxes

- When you need to select from a number of options, the options are often displayed in *list boxes*, and as you saw earlier, when more choices are available than can fit in the list box, the list box has a scroll bar. The list box we used earlier in the Date And Time dialog box presented a vertical list of words with a vertical scroll bar. In this Save As dialog box, the list has icons accompanied by words and no scroll bar. Regardless of the format of a list box, you select an option by clicking it. The option is then highlighted in the list.

Moving in a list

When a list box is active (one item in the list is selected), you can move the selection up or down one item at a time in the list by pressing the Up Arrow key or the Down Arrow key. You can move to the first or last item in the list by pressing Home or End. And you can press Page Up or Page Down to display the previous or next set of items.

- For space reasons, options are sometimes displayed in *drop-down list boxes*. Initially, a drop-down list appears as a box containing an option. To the right of the box is a downward-pointing arrow that you can click to drop down a list of other available options. To select an option, you simply click it. That option then appears in the collapsed list box. The Save As Type option at the bottom of the Save As dialog box is an example of a drop-down list box.

- Some options are presented with *check boxes* (small squares) in front of them. (You saw a check box at the beginning of the chapter, in the Welcome window.) Clicking an empty check box selects the associated option; a ✔ appears in the box to indicate that the option is active, or turned on. Clicking the box again removes the ✔ to indicate that the option is inactive, or turned off. Check boxes operate independently of one another, so if a dialog box presents a group of check boxes, you can select none, one, or all of the options, as required for the task at hand.

  Check boxes

- Other options are presented with *option buttons* (small circles). There are no option buttons in the dialog box now on your screen, but as you'll see later, these buttons always appear as a group of mutually exclusive options. When you click an option button, a black dot appears in the button to indicate that the option is active. Because only one option in the group can be active at a time, the black dot disappears from the button of the previously active option.

  Option buttons

- Most dialog boxes have at least two *command buttons*: one that closes the dialog box and carries out the command according to your specifications and one that closes the dialog box and cancels the command. Some dialog boxes have additional command buttons, which you can use to refine the original command. As with commands on menus, if the label on a button is followed by an ellipsis (...), clicking the button opens another dialog box. One command button (in this case, Save) usually has a heavy border around it to indicate that pressing Enter selects that button.

  Command buttons

- Some dialog boxes have settings that consist of a value in an edit box with a pair of up and down arrows, called *spinners,* at the right end. You change the setting either by typing a new value or by clicking the arrows to increase or decrease the value. Settings can also be represented by the position of a *slider* on a horizontal or vertical bar. To change the setting, you drag the slider.

  Spinners

  Sliders

- Some dialog boxes have toolbar buttons that let you interrupt the current task in order to carry out a different one or modify the current task in some way. The four buttons to the right of the Save In option are examples of this type of button.

In the Save As dialog box now on your screen, WordPad suggests *Document* as the name of the document in the File Name edit box. The Save In option at the top of the dialog box indicates that WordPad will save your document on the Windows desktop unless you specify otherwise. Take our word for it: Saving a document with a generic name and saving it on the desktop are both bad practices (see page 45). Instead, you want to give the document a unique descriptive name and tuck it in a predictable location with other related documents so that it will be easy to find weeks or even months from now. Follow these steps:

1. The word *Document* is selected in the File Name box, so simply type *Directions* to replace it.

2. Click the downward-pointing arrow to the right of the Save In option to drop down a hierarchical list of potential storage locations, something like this:

Moving dialog boxes

Moving dialog boxes

If you need to see the part of your document that is obscured by a dialog box, you can move the dialog box out of the way by dragging its title bar, the same way you would drag a window (see page 10).

Notice that this desktop has three storage locations: My Computer (your PC), Network Neighborhood (the PCs on any network to which you are connected), and My Briefcase. My Computer in turn has several storage locations, which, depending on your particular hardware configuration, might consist of one or more floppy drives, a hard drive, and perhaps a CD-ROM drive. If you are connected to a network, Network

Neighborhood might also include several storage locations, depending on which other computers are available to you.

3. Select the C: drive, which in our case is called *Hard_drive (C:)*, from the list. Hard_drive (C:) replaces Desktop in the Save In box, and the list box below changes to display a set of folders in which various files are already stored on your hard drive:

You could save the memo in the C: drive folder, but for the same reason you shouldn't save a document on the desktop, you shouldn't throw every document you create in one big folder and expect to be able to easily find a specific document later on. (See page 44 for further discussion.)

4. Click the Create New Folder button at the top of the dialog box to create this new folder within the C: drive folder:

The Create New Folder button

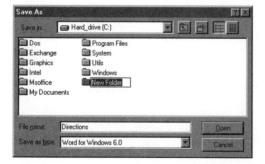

5. The title of the new folder is highlighted to indicate that it is selected. Type *Staff Party* to replace the selected title with a more descriptive one, and press Enter.

Name conventions

Filenames and folder names cannot have more than 255 characters, and they cannot contain these characters:

: * | \ < > " ? /

See page 44 for more advice about naming files and folders.

6. Now double-click the folder icon to the left of Staff Party to open the folder.

7. Click the downward-pointing arrow to the right of the Save As Type option and select Rich Text Format (RTF) from the drop-down list. Then click the Save command button to save the memo. The dialog box closes, and you return to the WordPad window, where *Directions* has replaced *Document* in the title bar and on the taskbar button.

Using Object Menus

Windows 95 programs make extensive use of object menus, which group together the commands you are most likely to use with a particular object. To display an object's menu, you point to the object and click with the right mouse button. (This technique is called *right-clicking*.) Try this:

Right-clicking

1. Choose the Select All command from the Edit menu to select the entire memo.

2. Move the pointer over the selection and click the right mouse button to display this object menu, which includes commands for manipulating the selected text:

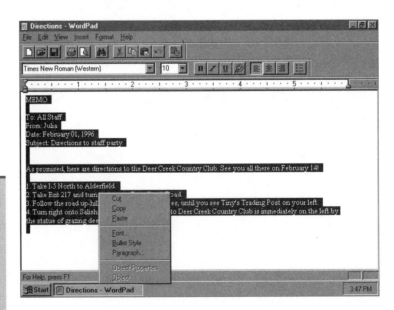

Changing your mind

If you change your mind about the settings you have made in a dialog box but can't remember what the settings were when you started, simply click Cancel to close the dialog box. You can then choose the command again and start all over if necessary.

3. Choose Paragraph to display this dialog box:

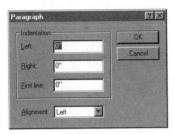

4. Type *1* to replace the highlighted 0 in the Left edit box, and then click the OK command button. Here's the result:

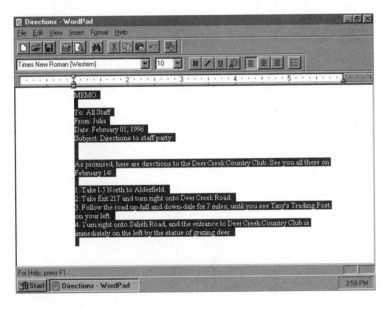

Choosing Commands with Toolbar Buttons

Many Windows programs come with one or more toolbars, which sport buttons and boxes that carry out common commands. Clicking a button carries out the corresponding command with its predefined, or *default*, settings. When you want to use a command with something other than its default settings, you must choose the command from its menu. To familiarize yourself with the buttons on the WordPad toolbar, follow the step on the next page.

Message boxes

Windows displays messages and warnings in message boxes when a command can't be carried out or there is a chance you might regret having chosen the command (for example, when deleting files). Clicking OK or Yes in a message box acknowledges the message and continues the command, whereas clicking Cancel or No cancels the command and closes the message box.

ToolTips

1. Point to each toolbar button in turn, pausing until the button's name appears in a box below the pointer. (A brief description of each button's function also appears in the status bar at the bottom of the WordPad window.) You can use this helpful feature, which is called *ToolTips*, to identify the buttons in most Windows programs.

To demonstrate how to use toolbar buttons, we'll show you a very important button. The 1-inch left indent you just set looks a bit goofy. You could repeat the previous set of steps to reverse the Paragraph command, but here's an easier way:

The Undo button

1. Click the Undo button on the toolbar (the equivalent of the Undo command on the Edit menu). WordPad resets the left indent to 0.

Many Windows programs include an Undo feature, enabling you to reverse your last editing action. Knowing that you can always take a step backward makes experimenting less hazardous, so it's worth checking out the Undo feature of your favorite programs. (That way, you'll know exactly what to do if you paint yourself into a corner.)

Quitting Programs

Quitting a program couldn't be easier. Follow these steps:

1. Click the Close button at the right end of the title bar. Because you have done some work since you last saved the document, WordPad displays this message box:

2. Click Yes to save the current version of Directions.

That's it! The WordPad window closes, it's button disappears from the taskbar, and you return to the desktop.

Getting Help

Using Windows is fairly intuitive, and this book will help you find your way around so that, most of the time, you will know exactly what to do and how. However, for those times when you stumble, Windows provides several ways to get the information you need. For example, to get information about an option in an open dialog box, you can click a Help button in the dialog box's title bar and then click the option you want to know about.

The Help button in dialog boxes

For those times when you need information about a particular operation, Windows provides a Help feature. Think of the Help feature as an encyclopedia-sized book that you can page through for help. Windows provides Help files for all its components, and most Windows programs provide them as well. Here's how to access the Windows Help system:

1. Click the Start button and choose Help from the Start menu to display this dialog box:

The Help contents

As you can see, the Help dialog box is multilayered, with each layer designated at the top of the dialog box by a tab like a file folder tab. The Contents tab is currently displayed. (If it's not, click Contents at the top of the dialog box.) This tab organizes help topics in broad categories.

Tabbed dialog boxes

2. Double-click the book icon to the left of *How To* to display a list of How To categories.

3. Double-click the book icon to the left of *Safeguard Your Work* to display a list of topics.

4. Double-click the question-mark icon to the left of *Shutting Down Your Computer* to display this topic window:

5. Read the information in the window and then click the Close button at the right end of the window's title bar.

To search for specific information in Help, follow these steps:

The Help index

1. Choose Help from the Start menu and click the Index tab to display these options:

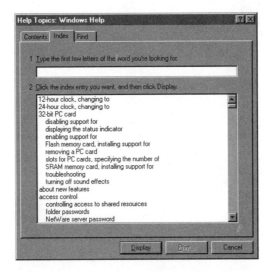

Help's hidden information

In some topics, clicking a short-cut button (a small gray button with an arrow) takes you from the topic directly to the dialog box in which you can perform the task you are inquiring about. Clicking a small gray button (without an arrow) takes you to a related topic. Clicking a word underlined with dots displays a pop-up definition of that word.

2. Type *shutt* in the edit box to scroll the list box below to the topics starting with those letters.

3. Click the Display button to display the topic window shown earlier.

4. Click the window's Close button.

When you can't locate the information you need using the Contents or Index tabs, which rely on topic headings, you can use the Find tab, which searches through the text of the topics. Before you can use this method of searching, you must use the Find Setup Wizard, which appears when you click the Find tab for the first time, to create a list of all the words in the topics. Thereafter, clicking the Find tab displays a dialog box in which you enter the word(s) for the topic you want to find, select matching words to narrow your search, and then select a topic and click Display.

The Help Find tab

When the topic you want is displayed, you can click the Options button and choose a command, for example, to annotate the topic with your own comments (see the tip below) or to print it. You can also specify that the Help window stay on top of any other windows you might open. You can click the Help Topics button to return to the Help dialog box without closing the topic window, and if you have several topic windows open, you can click the Back button to retrace your way back to where you started.

You might want to explore the Windows Help feature on your own for a while. When you've finished, rejoin us as we take you through the steps for turning off your computer.

Annotations

Choosing Annotate from Help's Options menu displays a text window in which you can add a note to the current Help topic for future reference. When you click Save to close the window, a small paperclip icon appears next to the topic name. Just click the icon to display your note.

When you need advice

In the US, the telephone number for Microsoft Product Support Services is (206) 635-7000. A message may instruct you to call an 800 number if you need sales and service. For questions about operating Windows, stay on the line and push the specified button to route your call to a Windows expert.

Shutting Down Your Computer

Well, this section is going to be easy, because you've already learned from the Windows Help feature how to turn off your computer. A word of warning: Never flip your computer's on/off switch without running through the shut-down procedure. Windows 95 does a lot of housekeeping at the end of each session to ensure that your computer will function properly the next time you turn it on. If you simply flip the switch, none of this housekeeping will get done, and there's no telling how future sessions might be affected. Here's how to shut down correctly:

1. Choose Shut Down from the Start menu. (It doesn't make sense to stop at the Start menu but you'll get used to it.) Windows displays the Shut Down Windows dialog box:

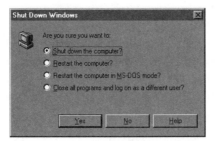

   This dialog box contains a set of option buttons that are fairly self-explanatory. (The last one applies only to computers that are on a network or have user profiles.) As we explained on page 17, option buttons are mutually exclusive; you can select only one of them.

2. With Shut Down The Computer selected, click Yes. Windows tidies everything up and tells you that you can turn off your computer.

If you tell Windows to shut down your computer without
closing an open program window, Windows closes it for you
as long as it does not contain a document with unsaved work
and as long as the program has completed its tasks. Otherwise,
the program gives you the chance to save the document before
it closes or displays a message telling you it can't quit. You
can then take the appropriate action before shutting down
your computer.

Closing open program
windows

Well, that's it for the quick tour. In the next chapter, we'll
focus on the documents you'll create with your Windows 95
programs.

2

Working with Documents

We show you how to track down and open existing documents using My Computer, Windows Explorer, and the Find command. Then you learn how to get organized by creating folders and moving, copying, renaming, and deleting documents.

Use My Computer to visually manage your folders and documents

Use Windows Explorer to organize your folders and documents in list format

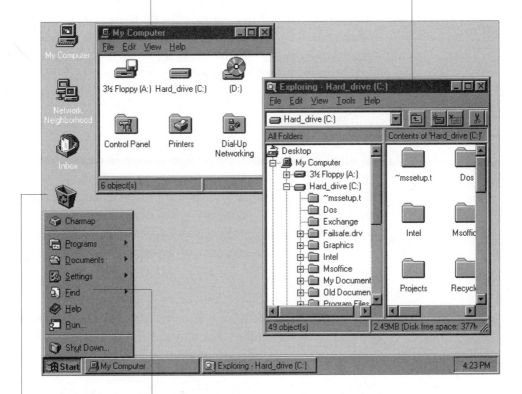

Remove unwanted folders and documents via the Recycle Bin

Locate folders and documents with the Find command

For some people, keeping computer files organized is a difficult chore. They'll load a program, start a new document, save it with a name such as Letter, and think they'll be able to retrieve the document without much trouble if they ever need it again. Because these people are busy, they often don't take the time to work out a file-naming system, and they may end up wasting a lot of time searching for the particular document they need. Is it Letter, or Smith Letter, or 1-12 Letter? And is it stored in the Letters folder, or the Smith folder, or the January folder?

With Windows 95, you no longer have to trust your memory to organize and retrieve documents efficiently. First, you can use up to 255 characters, including spaces, in a filename, so you can use filenames like Letter Written On 1-12-96 To Smith Associates About The Hunter Project to describe your documents. Second, Windows provides two organizational aids, My Computer and Windows Explorer, that you can use to shuffle your documents into folders in any way that makes sense to you.

In this chapter, we first show you how to find and open the documents you have created. Then we look at organizational strategies and techniques that you can use to make locating your documents as easy as possible.

Opening Recently Used Documents

In Chapter 1, you used WordPad to create a document called Directions. Suppose you now want to change some of the instructions in the document. Follow these steps to open it and make the changes:

Opening a document and a program simultaneously

1. Click the Start button to open the Start menu and then point to Documents. Windows displays a submenu of the documents you have worked on recently (up to a maximum of 15 documents), like this:

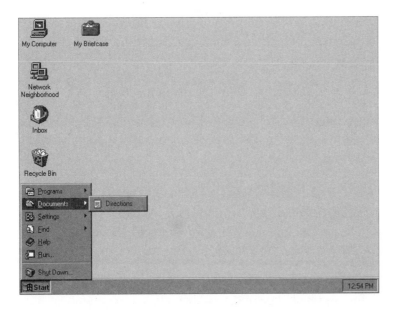

2. Move the pointer over the submenu to the document named Directions and click the left mouse button. Windows opens the document in a WordPad window so that you can begin editing.

Notice that you don't have to first start a program and then open the document.

Now let's change the memo slightly and save it with a different name so that we will have a couple of documents to play with:

1. In the first instruction, change the word *North* to *South*. (Click an insertion point after the *h* of *North*, press Backspace to erase the word, and then type *South*.)

2. In the second instruction, change the word *right* to *left*.

3. Choose Save As from the File menu to display the dialog box shown earlier on page 16, type *Directions From North* as the filename, leave all the other settings as they are, and click Save to save this new version of the document with a different name.

Windows knows which program to start

Windows 95 stores information about your system in its *registry*. Included in the registry is a list of programs on your computer and the types of documents they create, designated by a three-letter code called an *extension*. When you save a document, Windows attaches a hidden extension to the filename based on the Save As Type setting in the Save As dialog box. Later, Windows uses the extension to determine which program to start when you open the document.

4. Now click the Start button and point to Documents to display its submenu, which now includes Directions From North as well as the original Directions.

5. Click anywhere away from the menu to close it.

Multitasking

Notice that you don't have to close or minimize the document window in order to access the Start menu and do other types of work.

Clearing the Documents Submenu

Sometimes you might want to start a Windows session with an empty Documents submenu to avoid the clutter of old documents you don't need. Follow these steps to clear the submenu:

1. Point to a blank area of the taskbar, click the right mouse button, and choose Properties from the taskbar's object menu to display the Taskbar Properties dialog box, which has two tabs.

2. Click the Start Menu Programs tab to display these options:

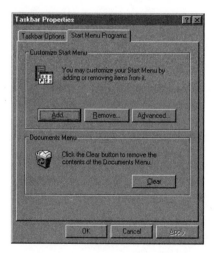

As you can see, buttons in the Customize Start Menu section enable you to add and remove commands from the Start menu (see page 63 for more information).

3. Click the Clear button in the Documents Menu section to remove the list of documents from the submenu, and then click OK to close the dialog box.

4. Click the Start button and point to Documents. As you can see here, the submenu has been cleared (the documents themselves are still safely stored on disk):

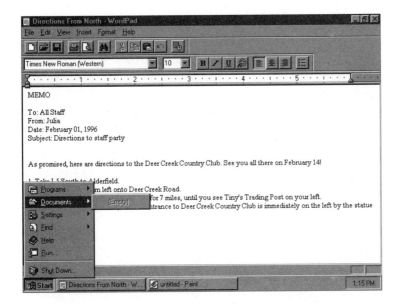

5. Press Esc three times to close the Documents submenu and the Start menu.

Closing menus without choosing a command

6. Now click the Close button to close the Directions From North window in preparation for the next section.

Finding Documents

You've just seen how to open a document you have recently worked on. But what if you need to retrieve a document that you worked on a while ago? In this section, we explore some other ways of finding and opening documents. But first, let's talk more about how documents are stored so that you will know where to start looking for your own documents when the time comes.

Storage Basics

When saving documents, you saw that the storage space in your computer is divided into logical groups. For simplicity, you can think of this division as taking place on five levels:

The desktop

- The *desktop* contains all the storage resources available to you while you are working.

Local and network storage

- The desktop is divided into your computer's storage, which we'll refer to as *local storage*, and the storage of any other computers available if you are connected to a network, which we'll refer to as *network storage*. Also at this level are the Recycle Bin, which holds objects you have deleted from both local and network storage during the current session, and (if it is installed) My Briefcase, which helps you coordinate the use of files on more than one computer. (For information about the Recycle Bin and Briefcase, see pages 54 and 53.)

Drives

- Your local storage is divided into chunks of space called *drives*, which are designated by unique, single letters followed by a colon. Most computers have one hard-disk drive, called C:, and one or two floppy-disk drives, called A: and B:. If you have access to any other drives, such as a CD-ROM drive, they are assigned other letters (D:, E:, and so on). If your computer is on a network, your network storage is divided into the drives in other computers, which are designated by the computers' names. Also at this level are three *system folders*: Control Panel (see page 114), Printers (see page 140), and Dial-Up Networking (see page 156).

Folders and subfolders

- Divisions within drives are called *folders*. Some folders have other folders, or *subfolders*, within them. (In this book, we use the term *folder* to mean any folder, designating folders within folders as *subfolders* only when the relationship between folders is important.)

Files

- The lowest level of storage space is *files*, and they can be divided into two main categories: program files and data files. *Program files* contain instructions to the computer to run programs, such as a word processor or a game, and they are usually written by programmers. *Data files* are the documents you create while running a program, such as a letter you write using a word processor.

For example, you might write a report called *4th Qtr 1995 Sales Report* and store it in a subfolder called *1995* within the folder called *Sales Reports* on the C: drive of your computer. Finding the document is a matter of knowing in which folder and on which drive it is stored and using either My Computer or Windows Explorer, two programs that come with Windows 95, to locate and open it. When you're hazy about the name of the document or its location, you can use the Find feature to track it down. We'll try finding a document using all these methods in the next three sections.

Using My Computer

My Computer is represented by an icon directly on the desktop because you will probably use it often for basic file-management operations. My Computer uses hierarchical windows to enable you to see the structure of your local storage and find the documents you need. The quickest way to become familiar with My Computer is to start using it, so follow these steps to find the Directions document, which is stored in the Staff Party folder on your C: drive:

My Computer

The My Computer icon

1. Double-click the My Computer icon to display the folder window shown on the next page and add the window's button to the taskbar.

Paths

Some dialog boxes ask for the *path* of a document, which you can think of as the document's address. This address starts with the drive and traces through folders to the document, separating each storage level from the previous one with a backslash (\). For example, *C:\Staff Party\Directions From North* is the path of the Directions From North document stored in the Staff Party folder on the C: drive.

To click or double-click?

Confused about when to click and when to double-click? The rule of thumb is to click when you want to select something and to double-click when you want to carry out an action. If that distinction is hazy, you can always click and wait to see if that accomplishes your goal. If it doesn't, double-click.

Finding My Computer

If you have several windows open on the desktop, or if a window is maximized, the My Computer icon may be hidden. To find it, simply move or minimize the open windows.

Don't worry if your window looks a bit different from this
one. Your window contains icons representing the configuration of your particular computer, and some of your icons may
have different names.

2. Double-click the icon for your C: drive to open its folder
   window and add its button to the taskbar.

3. Find the icon for the Staff Party folder (you may have to scroll
   the window) and double-click it to open its window and add
   its button to the taskbar. Three open folder windows are now
   stacked on your screen, which looks something like this:

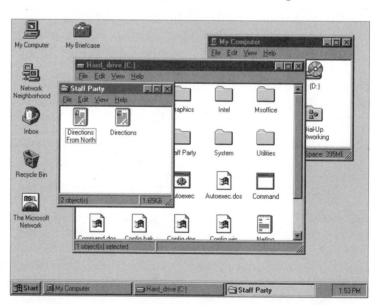

Shortcuts to folders

If you regularly use My Computer
to move to the same folder, you
might want to create a shortcut for
that folder. You can then simply
double-click the shortcut to jump
directly to the folder. For more
information about how to create
shortcuts, see page 59.

Notice that the title bar of the Staff Party window is a different
color than those of the windows beneath it, indicating that it
is the active window.

Having located the document, let's see how to open it:

1. Double-click the Directions icon to open the document in a WordPad window.

2. Use the Save As command to save a copy of the document with the name Directions From South. (Be sure the Save As Type box still displays Rich Text Format.)

3. Click the Close button to close the document, but leave the My Computer folder windows open.

You've probably noticed that folder windows are very similar to program windows (see page 8), except that, by default, they don't have toolbars. You move, size, minimize, maximize, restore, and close folder windows the same way you do program windows, and you choose commands from their menus the same way, too. Try this:

1. The Staff Party window should still be active. Click its Minimize button to hide the window under its button on the taskbar.

2. Click the My Computer button on the taskbar to bring that window to the top of the stack and make it active.

One folder window

Using separate folder windows for each level of storage can quickly clutter the screen. If you prefer, you can display successive levels in the same window, with each newly opened level replacing the previous one. Choose Options from a folder window's View menu, click the bottom option button on the Folder tab, and click OK. From then on, each folder you open is displayed in the active window. To redisplay the "parent" folder of the current folder, press Backspace.

Folder window toolbars

By default, toolbars are not displayed in folder windows. However, you can turn on the toolbar for the active window by choosing Toolbar from the View menu. (Other windows are not affected by this change.) Included on this toolbar are buttons that allow you to move up one level, reconfigure network settings, cut, copy, or paste folders and documents, undo a deletion, and change the display of the files in the window. (You may need to enlarge the window in order to view all of the buttons.)

Checking storage space

3. If necessary, click the C: drive icon to select it, and then take a look at the status bar at the bottom of the My Computer window. The status bar reports the number of objects selected and the capacity and amount of free space on your hard drive.

4. Minimize the My Computer window, leaving only the C: drive window open on the desktop.

5. Click an empty area of the window so that nothing is selected. The status bar of this window reports the number of objects (folders and files) in the window and the amount of space occupied by the files in the window:

The total storage space is for all the files in the window, including files hidden from view. (See the adjacent tip.) It does not include any files stored in subfolders of the C: drive folder.

Displaying all files

When you open some folder windows, Windows may not display files that are critical to its own or a particular program's operation. Because deleting or moving these files would create havoc, they are hidden from view. If you need to, you can display these files by choosing Options from the View menu, selecting Show All Files on the View tab, and clicking OK. Remember to reselect Hide Files Of These Types in the Options dialog box when you're done.

6. Click the Staff Party button on the taskbar to redisplay its window and then click the Directions From North icon. The size of the selected document is displayed in the status bar.

7. Choose Details from the View menu. Your view of the documents in the Staff Party folder changes to look like the one shown on the facing page. (We enlarged the window so that all the details are visible.)

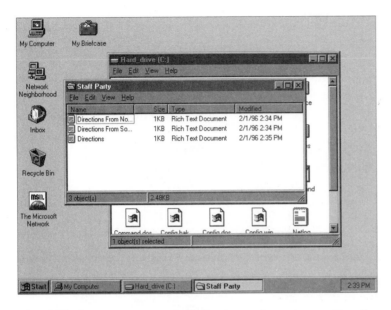

Now Windows reports each file's size and type, as well as the date each file was last modified. Notice that the contents of the C: drive window are still displayed as icons. You can change the view of one folder window independently of any others.

8. To open the Directions memo from this view, simply double-click the icon to the left of the document name. Then close the document again.

Opening documents from My Computer

We'll explore some of the other features and uses of My Computer later in this chapter. For now, let's close all the folder windows. You could close them one at a time, but we'll show you a quicker way. The windows now on your screen represent nested folders: Staff Party is within C:, which is, in turn, within My Computer. Here's how to close Staff Party, its "parent" C:, and its "grandparent" My Computer with just one click:

1. Hold down the Shift key and click the Close button of the Staff Party window. Windows first closes the active window, then closes the C: window, and then closes the minimized My Computer window.

Other views

In addition to the large-icon and details views we show here, you can view the contents of a folder window as a set of small icons or as a list, by choosing the corresponding command from the View menu. If you have turned on the folder window's toolbar (see the tip on page 37), you can use buttons to switch between views. (You may need to enlarge the window in order to display all of the toolbar buttons.)

Using Windows Explorer

Windows Explorer could be called *My Computer Plus*. To see why, start the program now:

1. Click the Start button and choose Programs and then Windows Explorer from the Start menu to display this window:

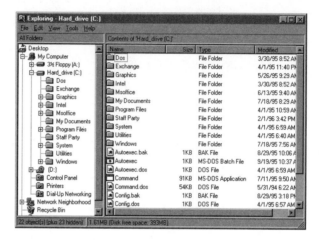

Notice that the pane on the right looks similar to the details view of a folder window displayed via My Computer.

The Large Icons button

2. Choose Toolbar from the View menu to display the toolbar, and then click the Large Icons button. Now the similarity is even more pronounced:

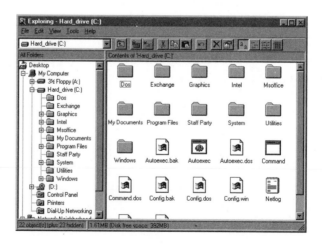

The most obvious difference between My Computer and Windows Explorer is the addition of the left pane, which displays a hierarchical diagram of all your available storage space arranged like this:

- At the top is the desktop.

The Windows Explorer diagram

- One level to the right are My Computer, Network Neighborhood, the Recycle Bin, and My Briefcase (if you are using it).

- One more level to the right are the available drives and the system folders (Control Panel, Printers, and Dial-Up Networking).

- One level to the right of your C: drive are all the folders contained in that drive's folder.

You can expand and contract the diagram, displaying only the highest levels or zooming in for a closer look at folders, subfolders, and files. Let's take a moment to experiment in the left pane:

1. Double-click the C: drive icon. The folder icons disappear (collapse), and the minus symbol to the left of the C: drive icon becomes a plus symbol, indicating that the drive contains hidden folders. Because the C: drive is still selected, its folders are displayed in the window's right pane even though they are no longer visible in the left pane, as shown here:

Collapsing the diagram

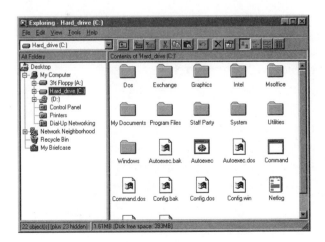

Expanding the diagram

2. Double-click the C: drive icon again. The folder icons reappear (expand), and the plus symbol reverts to a minus symbol, indicating that the folders it contains are not hidden.

3. Click the Windows folder icon in the diagram to display its contents in the right pane without displaying its contents in the left pane.

You can also change the display by double-clicking icons in the right pane. Try this:

1. Double-click the Cursors folder in the right pane. Windows Explorer opens the folder and displays its contents.

The Up One Level button

2. Click the Up One Level button on the toolbar to move back to the Windows folder, and then click the button again to display the contents of the C: drive folder.

Experiment with moving around in Windows Explorer until you are familiar with the various techniques for displaying the contents of folders and the various views you can assign to the right pane. Then rejoin us and follow these steps to open a document from Windows Explorer:

Opening documents from Windows Explorer

1. Display the contents of the Staff Party folder.

2. Double-click the Directions icon to open the document in WordPad. Then close the document again.

3. End this brief tour of Windows Explorer by clicking the Close button to close its window.

Using the Find Command

The third method of locating a document you want to open is to use the Find command on the Start menu. Searches performed with this command can be pretty sophisticated, but the vast majority of searches are simple attempts to locate a document based on all or part of its name. We'll show you how to conduct this type of search and leave you to explore further on your own, using the Find window's Help system if necessary. Let's get going:

Complex searches

In addition to searching for a document by name and location, you can search by modification date (when it was last saved), by file type, and by size. You can even search the content of your documents for a particular word or phrase. For example, you could search for a Word document that you saved between January 4 and January 14, 1996 and that contains the words *Deer Creek Country Club*.

1. With all windows closed, click the Start button, point to Find on the Start menu, and then choose Files Or Folders to display this window:

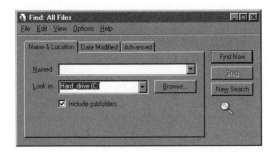

2. In the Named edit box, type *Directions*, leave all the other options as they are, and click the Find Now button to start the search. Windows searches all the subfolders within your C: drive folder, and here's the result:

Finding specific files

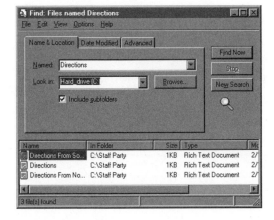

As you can see, Windows finds all the files whose names include the word *Directions*. You can change the view and manipulate the results of the search in various ways using the commands on the Find window's menus, and you can open the document you want from this window in the usual way:

1. Double-click the icon to the left of the Directions document's name to open the document in WordPad. Then close the document again.

2. Click the Close button of the Find window to close the window.

Finding other things

You can also use the Find command to search a network for a computer and, if you are working on The Microsoft Network, to search for particular objects in this online service's huge "library" of resources. (See page 164 for a brief discussion of The Microsoft Network.)

Organizing Folders and Documents

As you have seen, using icons to perform common operations makes them less intimidating than having to remember commands. So the real strength of Windows 95 becomes apparent when you use it to organize your folders and files by moving, copying, and deleting them.

Before you practice creating folders and moving documents, you might want to make a few decisions about what your folder and document structure should look like. When Windows 95 was installed on your computer, various folders were created on your hard drive to hold all the Windows documents. When you install a program under Windows 95, that program will probably also create folders. Our concern here is not with these program folders. In fact, unless you really know what you're doing, it is probably best to leave these program folders alone. Our concern is instead with the folders you will create to hold your own documents.

Because you can use long folder names and filenames in Windows 95, you might think it would be easy to name documents so that they are readily identifiable later. And there's no question that being able to use several words helps. Gone are the days when you had to convey the content of a

Short filenames

Long filenames work fine as long as you do all your work with Windows 95 programs, but if you are still using programs designed to run under Windows or Windows for Workgroups 3.*x*, or under DOS, you need to think carefully about the filenames you assign in Windows 95. For example, suppose you create a document in the Windows 95 version of Word and call it 1996 Product Brochure. You later need to open the document in Corel Ventura 5.0, a page-layout program designed to run under Windows 3.1 that can only handle eight-character filenames. When you look for the document from Ventura, you'll see the filename 1996PR~1.DOC. Windows has converted the filename successfully, filling in the space, using a tilde (~) to indicate that it has truncated the name, and adding the normally hidden extension (see the tip on page 31). The problem is that you may have several documents with long filenames that start with the same eight characters (1996 Product List, 1996 Product Reviews, 1996 Product Proposals, and so on). To distinguish these documents, Windows adds a number to each filename (1996_PR~1.DOC, 1996_PR~2.DOC, and so on) at which point it becomes hard to know at a glance which document is which. So if you need to work with documents in both Windows 95 and non-Windows 95 programs, try to assign filenames that will work well in both environments. (You can see what the short filename will be by right-clicking the document in My Computer or Windows Explorer, choosing Properties, and checking the MS-DOS Name setting.)

document with a filename of no more than eight characters. Nevertheless, coming up with a few rules for naming files is a must. If you have ever wasted time trying to locate a document, you will probably find that spending a few minutes now deciding how to avoid such incidents in the future will more than repay you in increased efficiency. And a file-naming convention is a must if more than one person in your workgroup works with the same set of documents.

Deciding on a System

However you decide to set up your folder structure, we strongly recommend that you store all the folders and documents you create in a folder called My Documents. (Depending on which programs are installed on your computer, you may already have a My Documents folder in your C: drive folder.) This precaution greatly simplifies the backing up of all your work (see page 94 for more information). We also recommend that, to the extent possible, you use some unique document identifier at the beginning of each filename, especially if the document is likely to be used with a non-Windows 95 program that can only handle eight-character filenames (see the tip on the facing page).

Using a My Documents folder

Using unique document identifiers

Otherwise, there are no hard and fast rules for organizing documents, and the scheme you come up with will depend on the nature of your work. For example, if your documents are client-based, it makes sense to identify them by client. You might use a client's name as the first word of the filename of every document connected with that account, follow the word with a date, and finish up by identifying the type of document. Thus, a filename like Smith 1-20 Letter might designate a letter written to Smith Associates on January 20, and the filename Smith 2-14 Invoice might designate an invoice sent to the same client a few weeks later.

The important thing is to come up with a simple scheme and to apply it consistently. You can then use Windows to manipulate the documents individually and in groups. For example, suppose you have accumulated so many documents in your client folders that you need to subdivide your client documents by type to make the documents more manageable.

Keep it simple

In an eagerness to impose structure, some people go overboard, developing convoluted naming systems and subfolder mazes in which it is easy to get lost. The result is usually as bad as no system at all, because it is less hassle to create filenames on the fly and search a huge folder than it is to remember how the system works. Remember, to take advantage of the file-organization capabilities of Windows, keep your system simple.

You can create a subfolder called Invoices, select all the documents in the client folder that have Invoice as part of their filename, and drag all the invoice documents to the new folder. In the following sections, we'll demonstrate organizational tasks like this one by using My Computer. Bear in mind, though, that you can use Windows Explorer just as easily.

Creating New Folders

You already saw in Chapter 1 how to create a new folder while saving a document (see page 19). Now we're going to create a new subfolder in the Staff Party folder for the Directions documents you've created in this chapter. Follow these steps:

1. Close all open windows, start My Computer by double-clicking its icon on the desktop, and open the Staff Party folder, which is on your C: drive.

2. With the Staff Party window active, choose New and then Folder from the File menu to display a new folder icon within the Staff Party window.

Naming folders ➤ 3. With the new folder selected, type *Directions* and press Enter.

4. Click the C: drive button on the taskbar to activate the C: drive window. If you do not have a My Documents subfolder in your C: drive folder, choose New and then Folder from the File menu and create that folder now.

> ### Arranging icons
>
> If you create several new folders or move/copy several folders and documents, folder windows can get pretty untidy, making particular objects hard to find. To straighten up the active folder, choose Arrange Icons and then By Name from the View menu. (You can also arrange by type, size, and date.) Windows puts your folders first, followed by your documents. Choose Arrange Icons and then Auto Arrange to have Windows do this bit of housekeeping every time you make a change to the folder's contents.

5. Close the My Computer and C: drive windows to reduce screen clutter, leaving the Staff Party window open.

Specifying What You Want to Work With

Having created the new folder, we're ready to select the documents we want to move or copy into it. You've already seen how to click an icon to select it. Here, we'll show you a few other ways:

1. Click the first document icon, hold down the Shift key, click the last document icon, and release Shift. The entire set of

documents is now selected. In the status bar, the number of selected documents and their total size is displayed, as shown below:

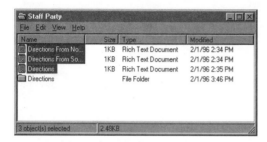

2. Hold down the Ctrl key, click the Directions icon, and release Ctrl. That icon is no longer part of the selection.

3. Click Directions. Now only that icon is selected.

4. Choose Invert Selection from the Edit menu to deselect the selected icon and select the other icons in the window. (This command deselects everything that was selected and selects everything that wasn't.)

Inverting selections

5. Click an empty area of the window to deselect everything.

Moving and Copying Folders and Documents

As a demonstration, we are going to move the Staff Party folder into the My Documents folder and then copy documents from the Staff Party folder to the new Directions subfolder. Follow these steps:

1. Open the C: drive window and make sure you can see both the My Documents and Staff Party folders. (Maximize the window if you can't.)

2. Select Staff Party, and using the *right* mouse button, drag the dotted image of the selected folder's icon over the My Documents icon. (The destination icon changes color when the pointer is in the correct place.) When you release the mouse button, you see the object menu shown on the next page.

Shift vs. Ctrl

When selecting objects in a folder window or Windows Explorer, holding down Shift while clicking extends the selection to include all the objects up to the object you clicked last. For example, if the second object is selected, holding down Shift and clicking the fourth object extends the selection to include the second, third, and fourth objects. Holding down Ctrl while clicking adds only the clicked object to the selection. For example, if the second object is selected, holding down Ctrl and clicking the fourth object adds the fourth object so that the second and fourth objects are selected but not the third. Holding down Ctrl while clicking a selected object removes that object from the selection without deselecting anything else.

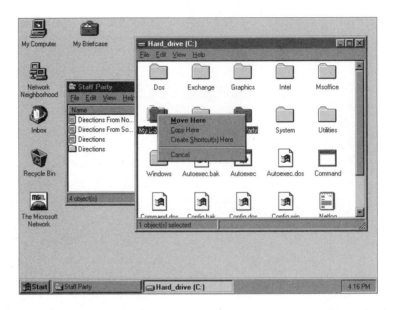

3. Choose Move Here to move the folder and its contents. The Staff Party icon disappears from the C: drive window, and the Staff Party window disappears from the desktop.

4. To verify that the folder and its documents have actually moved, open the My Documents folder:

Quick-viewing documents

If Windows 95 was installed on your machine from CD-ROM, you may be able to view a document before opening it, depending on what kind of document it is. Right-click the document in a folder window or Windows Explorer and then choose Quick View from the object menu to display the document in a Quick View window. (The command does not appear on the object menu if the document can't be viewed.) You can then open the document by clicking the Open File For Editing button on the window's toolbar.

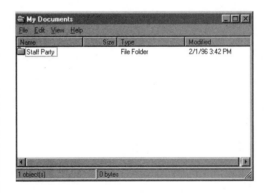

Next we'll move one of the documents to the new Directions folder, and then we'll copy another document:

1. Open the Staff Party folder and select Directions From North.

2. Using the *left* mouse button, drag the dotted image of the selected icon over the Directions folder. The Direction From North icon disappears from the Staff Party window.

3. Select Directions From South, hold down the Ctrl key, and using the *left* mouse button, drag the dotted image of the selected icon over the Directions folder. (As you drag, a plus sign is displayed below the pointer to indicate that you are copying the document, not moving it.) Release the Ctrl key and the mouse button. This time, the selected document's icon remains in the Staff Party window.

4. Click the Directions folder icon to display its window, and verify that the moved and copied documents are safely stored in their new folder:

Here's how to copy a document within the same folder:

1. Click the Directions From North icon in the Directions window to select it.

2. Choose Copy from the Edit menu. Windows puts a copy of the document on the Clipboard, a temporary storage place in your computer's memory.

3. Choose Paste from the Edit menu. Windows pastes a copy of the Clipboard's contents back into the Directions window, naming the new document Copy Of Directions From North.

You can use this same technique to copy documents from one folder to another. Try this:

1. Activate the Staff Party window, select the Directions document icon, and choose Copy from the Edit menu.

2. Switch to the Directions window and choose Paste from the Edit menu. As you can see on the next page, you now have four documents in this folder.

The Clipboard

The Windows Clipboard is a temporary storage place in your computer's memory in which cut or copied data from all Windows programs is stored. You can use it to transfer data within the same program or from one program to another (see page 74). Each object you cut or copy overwrites the previous object. Because the Clipboard is a temporary storage place, shutting down your computer erases any information you have stored there.

Copying Documents to and from Floppy Disks

If you work on more than one computer or share documents with colleagues but you are not hooked up to a network, you will need to copy documents to and from floppy disks to get the documents from one computer to another. You might also want to copy documents to floppy disks as a means of backing up your work (see page 94 for more information). The first step in copying documents to a floppy disk is to insert a formatted disk in the appropriate drive, so let's take a detour to discuss how to format floppy disks. To practice formatting, find a floppy disk that is either new or that contains information you don't mind losing (formatting destroys any data already stored on the disk) and then follow these steps:

1. Minimize the Directions window and close any other open windows except My Computer. If My Computer is not already open, double-click its icon on the desktop.

2. Insert a disk in the floppy drive and right-click the drive's icon in the My Computer window to display its object menu.

3. Choose Format from the menu to display this dialog box:

Moving and copying with Windows Explorer

To move and copy files in Windows Explorer, you use the same techniques as in My Computer, except that you work between panes. For example, to move the Staff Party folder into the My Documents folder, you would first double-click the C: drive folder in the left pane to display its contents in the right pane. Then in the right pane, you would drag the Staff Party folder icon over the My Documents folder icon. To copy the Directions From South document from the Staff Party folder to the Directions folder, you would double-click the Staff Party folder in the left pane, hold down the Ctrl key, and in the right pane, drag the Directions From South icon over the Directions folder icon.

4. Check that the value in the Capacity box is correct for the disk you are formatting. (You can select a different capacity from the drop-down list.)

5. If this disk has never been formatted before, select Full in the Format Type section. Also select this type of format if you want to be sure that the disk contains no bad sectors.

6. Leave the other options as they are and click Start. Windows quickly formats the disk, displaying its progress in the bar at the bottom of the dialog box.

7. When formatting is complete, Windows displays information about the storage capacity of the disk and the number of bytes in bad (unusable) sectors, if any. Click Close to close this message box, and then close the Format dialog box.

You are now ready to copy the Directions documents to the formatted disk. But first, let's unclutter the screen:

1. Right-click a blank area of the taskbar and choose Minimize All Windows from its object menu. All the open windows are now hidden under their buttons on the taskbar.

2. Click the My Computer button and the Directions button to redisplay those two windows, and then arrange the windows so that you can see the floppy drive icon in the My Computer window when the Directions window is active.

3. With the Directions window active, choose Select All from the Edit menu to select all four documents, point to one of the selected icons, and using the *left* mouse button, drag the selection over the floppy drive icon in the My Computer window. Release the mouse button. While Windows copies the documents, it displays a progress box with documents flying from one folder to another.

4. Verify that the documents have been copied by displaying the floppy drive's window, as shown on the next page.

Creating a system disk

A system disk contains the files necessary to "boot" (start) your computer. To create a system disk, follow the steps for formatting a floppy disk and in the Format dialog box, select Full in the Format Type section (to ensure that the disk has no bad sectors) and Copy System Files in the Other Options section, and then click Start. You can then use this disk to start your computer in Windows 95 if anything ever attacks your hard drive. (By the way, if you created a startup disk while installing Windows 95, use this disk instead; it contains diagnostic programs in addition to the system files necessary to start your computer. If you don't have a startup disk but would like one, see page 92.)

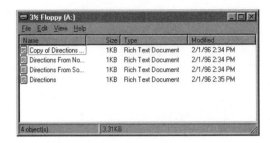

5. Remove the disk and put it to one side for now. (You will use it again later in this book.)

You can copy files in the other direction (from a floppy disk to a folder on your hard disk) using the technique we just described.

Renaming Folders and Documents

During the course of your work, you will sometimes want to change a filename. For example, suppose you want all the filenames of the documents in the Directions folder to start with a unique word. Try these four methods of renaming the documents:

1. Close or minimize the open windows and then display the Directions window.

2. Right-click the Directions document icon, choose Rename from the object menu, type *West Directions* as the new name, and press Enter.

3. Select the Copy Of Directions From North icon, choose Rename from the window's File menu, type *East Directions*, and press Enter.

4. Select the Directions From North icon, press the F2 key, type *North Directions*, and press Enter.

5. Finally, select the Directions From South icon, wait a second, then point to its name and click again to activate the name, type *South Directions*, and press Enter. Here are the results:

Copying vs. moving

When you use the left mouse button to drag a folder or document to a new location on the same drive, Windows moves the object, unless you hold down the Ctrl key, in which case it copies the object. When you use the left mouse button to drag between drives, Windows also copies the object, whether you hold down the Ctrl key or not. If you find this logic confusing, use the right mouse button to drag so that you can choose the correct action from the object menu.

You can also use any of these methods to rename folders.

Deleting and Undeleting Folders and Documents

If you followed along with the previous examples, you now have two extraneous documents in the Staff Party folder. The potential for confusion is obvious, so let's throw out the duplicate documents in the Staff Party folder:

1. Close or minimize all windows and then open the Staff Party window.

2. Select the Directions *document* icon and press the Delete key.

3. When Windows asks you to confirm the deletion, click Yes.

4. Right-click the Directions From South icon and choose Delete from its object menu.

5. Again, confirm the deletion when prompted.

That's it! Both documents are gone.

You can use either of these techniques to delete a folder, its subfolders, and its documents with a couple of mouse clicks. A great shortcut, you might think. But it's wise to inspect the contents of not only the folder you are considering deleting but also all its subfolders before carrying out this type of wholesale destruction.

Fortunately, Windows provides a safeguard against the nightmare of inadvertently deleting vital documents. When you use Windows to delete objects from your hard disk or the desktop, Windows doesn't really delete them. Instead, it moves them to a folder on your hard disk called the Recycle

Using the Briefcase

If you use more than one computer (for example, a desktop machine in the office and a laptop at home or on the road) instead of simply copying documents to a floppy disk to transfer them from one computer to another, you will want to use the Briefcase. This feature of Windows 95 coordinates documents so that you don't wind up with one version on one computer and another version on a different computer and no way of merging the two without tedious manual work. The details of the Briefcase are beyond the scope of this book, but if your work situation involves using more than one computer, you will probably want to explore this feature further.

Bin. Until you empty the bin, you can retrieve objects you have deleted by mistake. Try this:

1. Choose Undo Delete from the window's Edit menu to restore Directions From South to the Staff Party window.

You could repeat this step to undelete Directions, but instead let's go rummaging in the Recycle Bin:

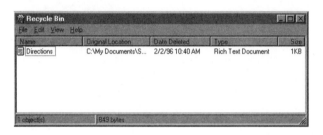

Recycle Bin

The Recycle Bin icon ▶ 1. Double-click the Recycle Bin on the desktop to display its window as shown below. (We enlarged the window to show all the details.)

Recycle Bin				□ ×
File Edit View Help				
Name	Original Location	Date Deleted	Type	Size
Directions	C:\My Documents\S...	2/2/96 10:40 AM	Rich Text Document	1KB
1 object(s)	849 bytes			

How big is the Recycle Bin?

To check the size of your computer's Recycle Bin, right-click its icon and choose Properties from the object menu. By default, the bin occupies 10 percent of the hard drive on which it is stored, but you can adjust the size by moving the slider to the left (smaller) or right (bigger). If you have more than one hard drive, Windows maintains a bin on each drive. Click the drive tab(s) to see how big the bin is on a particular drive. To set different bin sizes for each drive, click the Configure Drives Independently option on the Global tab before adjusting the slider on each tab.

Restoring folders

Did you delete an entire folder and now want to restore one of its documents? No problem. Although the folder is not in the Recycle Bin, the documents, and a record of their original location, are. Restore the documents in the usual way. Windows will automatically recreate the folder.

Deleting without recycling

If you know you will never need a document that is stored on your hard drive again, you can delete it permanently by holding down the Shift key while pressing Delete. Documents deleted from network drives and floppy drives are always deleted permanently rather than being moved to the Recycle Bin. So always think carefully before confirming deletions from these drives.

2. Right-click Directions and then choose Restore from the object menu.

3. Close the Recycle Bin window.

Now let's delete both documents again:

1. With the Staff Party window active, make sure you can see the Recycle Bin icon on the left side of the desktop.

2. Select the Directions document icon, hold down the Ctrl key, and click Directions From South to add it to the selection.

3. Point to a selected icon and drag the selection over the Re-cycle Bin icon. When you release the mouse button, Windows removes the documents from the Staff Party window.

If you run out of space in your Recycle Bin, you can empty it. Follow these steps to remove documents from the bin and completely erase them from your hard disk:

1. Double-click the Recycle Bin icon to open its window.

Emptying the Recycle Bin

2. Select Directions in the list box, press the Delete key, and then click Yes to confirm that you want to permanently remove the document.

3. Now choose Empty Recycle Bin from the File menu to erase the remaining contents of the bin, clicking Yes to confirm your command.

4. Close all the open windows.

If you are sure you won't need to restore any of the documents in the Recycle Bin, you can empty it without checking it by right-clicking its icon and choosing Empty Recycle Bin from the object menu. Click Yes to confirm your command.

In this long chapter, we have given you an overview of the tools Windows 95 offers to help you get organized so that you can quickly find your documents. Now it's up to you!

3 Increasing Your Efficiency

We create handy shortcut icons on the desktop and add shortcuts to the Start menu. Then using Word-Pad, Calculator, Character Map, and Paint, we show you how to multitask and recycle information from one program to another.

Create shortcut icons to quickly access programs and documents

Run multiple programs at the same time

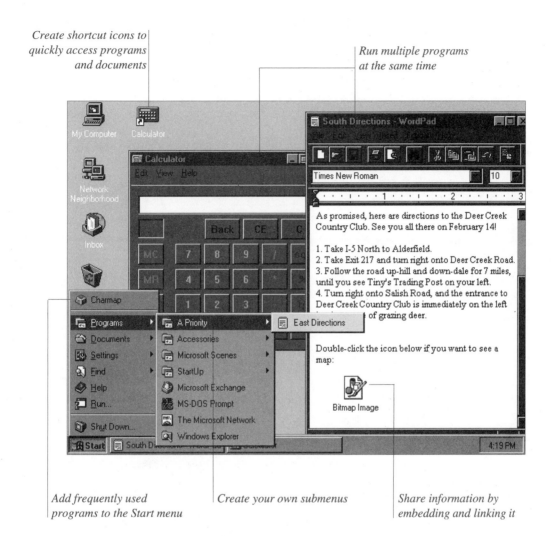

Add frequently used programs to the Start menu

Create your own submenus

Share information by embedding and linking it

Chapters 1 and 2 showed you how to accomplish basic Windows 95 tasks and gave you enough information to start working in this new environment. By now you've probably experimented a bit, and you're ready to move on to more complex tasks. In this chapter, we focus on how to take advantage of Windows 95 to get your work done efficiently.

Windows programs ───────────►

Windows 95 comes with a grab bag of indispensable utilities and programs, some that are quite large and involved (such as WordPad and Paint) and others that are small and simple (such as Calculator and Character Map). In this chapter, we'll use a few of them to demonstrate basic techniques for working with Windows programs. We won't describe these programs in any detail because our focus is on the techniques, not the programs. But we will tell you enough to get you going; you can then experiment with specific programs on your own.

Accessing Programs and Documents Quickly

You've learned how to start a program by choosing it from the Programs submenu of the Start menu. You've also learned how to start a program and open a document at the same time using the following methods:

- Choosing a document from the Documents submenu of the Start menu.

- Double-clicking a document in the My Computer, Windows Explorer, or Find window. (You can also start a program by double-clicking its icon in these windows.)

Missing program?

If you can't find a Windows program used in our examples, the program may not be installed on your computer. You can easily install a missing Windows program by choosing Settings and then Control Panel from the Start menu and following the instructions on page 118.

All of these methods of getting down to work require several steps, but with Windows 95, you can speed things up by making the programs and documents you use most frequently immediately accessible. In this section, we'll examine two simple techniques to provide instant access. Along the way, we'll introduce a couple of the programs that come with Windows, and you'll practice basic skills you learned in the previous chapters.

Creating Shortcut Icons

For the ultimate in convenience, you can create a shortcut icon to any program, folder, or document and place it on the desktop. Then double-clicking the icon starts the program, or takes you directly to the folder's window, or opens the document, depending on the nature of the shortcut.

To demonstrate, we'll use Calculator, the handy number-cruncher that is shipped with Windows. Follow these steps:

1. Double-click My Computer on the desktop and then choose Options from the View menu to display this dialog box:

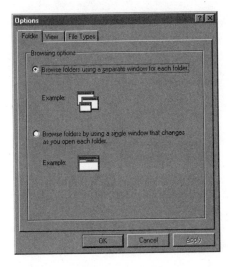

2. To have Windows display the contents of all folders in one window instead of opening a separate window for each folder, select the bottom (single-window) option and click OK.

3. In the My Computer window, double-click the C: drive icon to display its contents in the window, and then double-click the Windows icon to display its subfolders and files.

4. Scroll the window to find the Calc (for *Calculator*) program.

5. Point to the Calc icon, and using the *right* mouse button, drag the dotted image of the icon up and onto the desktop, releasing the mouse button when the image is to the right of the My Computer icon.

Using a single window

Creating shortcut icons for programs

6. Choose Create Shortcut(s) Here from the object menu. Windows adds the shortcut icon shown below to the desktop. (You might have to rearrange some of the other icons on the desktop to see the shortcut icon.)

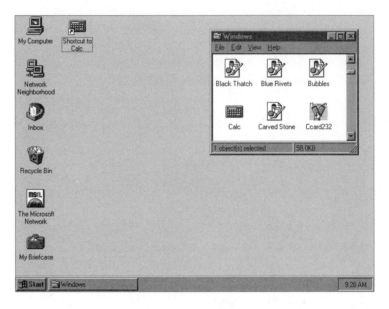

Changing icon names

7. The arrow in the bottom left corner of the icon tells you that double-clicking this icon is a shortcut for starting the program called Calc, so you don't need the word *Shortcut* in the name. To change the name, click the icon to select it, wait a second and then click the icon name, type Calculator, and press Enter.

Now let's try out the shortcut icon:

Using Calculator

1. Double-click the Calculator shortcut icon to start the program and display this window:

2. Click the buttons for 14.95, click *, click the 4 button, and then click =. (You can also press numeric keypad keys.) The display bar shows the cost (without sales tax) of four copies of *A Quick Course in Windows 95*: 59.8, or $59.80.

3. Close the Calculator by clicking its Close button.

Creating a shortcut icon to a folder or document is just as easy. As an example, let's put the Directions folder and the Directions From North documents within easy reach:

1. With the Windows folder window active, press Backspace until the C: drive icon is displayed. Double-click the icon and then navigate through the My Documents folder to the Staff Party folder.

2. Using the right mouse button, drag the Directions folder icon to the desktop, (choose Create Shortcut(s) Here from the object menu), and change the name of the shortcut to Directions. Here are the results:

Creating shortcut icons for folders and documents

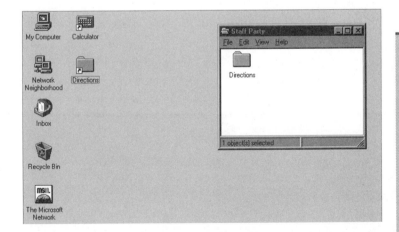

Tidying the desktop

After you've added a few short-cuts to the desktop, things can start to get a bit messy. You can straighten up the desktop by right-clicking a blank area of the desktop and choosing Line Up Icons. Windows keeps the icons in the order in which you've placed them but arranges them in neat rows and columns. You can have Windows automatically arrange icons in columns, starting at the left edge of the screen, by choosing Arrange Icons and then Auto Arrange from the desktop's object menu. (Choosing any of the Arrange Icons subcommands overrides any order you have established by manually moving the icons.)

3. Double-click the Directions shortcut icon. Windows opens the folder's window without going through any preceding folder levels.

4. Using the right mouse button, drag the North Directions document icon to the desktop, (choose Create Shortcut(s) Here from the object menu), and change the shortcut icon's name to North Directions.

5. Double-click the North Directions shortcut icon. Windows starts WordPad and opens the document. Click the Close button to close the window again.

Creating shortcut icons in folders

You can create shortcut icons within folders as well as on the desktop. For example, to create a shortcut icon in the C: drive folder to the North Directions document, you would display the C: drive and Directions folder windows, right-drag the North Directions icon from the Directions window into the C: drive window, and choose Create Shortcut(s) Here from the object menu.

Deleting Shortcut Icons

When you no longer need immediate access to a program, folder, or document, you can delete its shortcut icon to free up space on the desktop. Here's how:

1. Select the North Directions shortcut icon on the desktop and press the Delete key.

2. When Windows asks you to confirm that you really want to send the North Directions shortcut icon to the Recycle Bin, click Yes.

3. Close any open windows.

The Create Shortcut Wizard

In our example, we select an object and then specify the location for its shortcut icon. But you can also select a location and then specify the object. Simply right-click the desktop or the folder where you want to create the shortcut icon and choose New and then Shortcut from the object menu. Windows starts the Create Shortcut Wizard, and you can then follow the instructions on page 64.

Program icons vs. shortcut icons

Shortcut icons are distinguished from program icons by the upward pointing arrow in the bottom left corner. Whereas program icons identify the storage locations of the programs they represent (like the numbers on a house or a sign on a building), shortcut icons are instructions to Windows. For example, the program icon for the Calculator is located in the Windows folder on your C: drive if that's where the program is stored, and if you move the program to another folder, its icon moves to the new location, too. However, if you create a shortcut icon to the Calculator on the desktop, the icon doesn't indicate that the program is stored on the desktop. Instead, it stores the address of the program, and double-clicking the icon tells Windows to go to that address and start the program it finds there. Each program has only one program icon, but you can create as many shortcuts to that program as you want. And when you no longer need a shortcut, you can delete it without affecting the program or its other shortcuts in any way.

Adding and Removing Start Menu Shortcuts

When you are working in a maximized window, you cannot see the desktop to double-click any shortcut icons you might have placed there. In that case, you will find it quicker to access a program or document from the Start menu.

The Start menu is actually a group of shortcuts arranged in a series of submenus. You can add shortcuts to the Start menu itself or to its Programs submenu. Follow these steps:

1. Double-click the My Computer icon on the desktop to open its window, double-click the C: drive icon, and then double-click the Windows icon.

2. Scroll the Windows window to find the Charmap (for *Character Map*) application file. (Later in the chapter, you'll learn how to use the Character Map.)

3. Point to the Charmap icon, and using the *left* mouse button, drag the dotted image of the icon down onto the Start button in the bottom left corner of the screen.

Adding programs to the Start menu

4. Now click the Start button. As you can see here, the Character Map is now accessible from the Start menu:

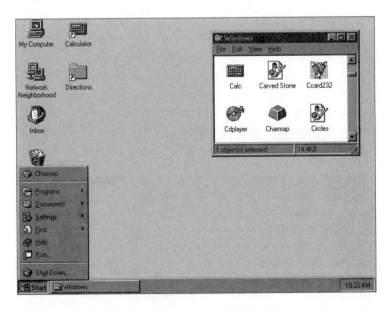

5. Close the Windows window.

Suppose you want to create a submenu from which you can easily access all the important documents you are currently working on, including the Directions documents. Here's how to add this submenu to the Start menu's Programs list and add a shortcut for the East Directions document to the submenu:

Adding submenus to the Start menu

1. Right-click a blank area of the taskbar, choose Properties from the object menu, and click the Start Menu Programs tab in the Taskbar Properties dialog box to display the options shown earlier on page 32.

2. Click the Add button. Windows starts the Create Shortcut Wizard, which displays this dialog box:

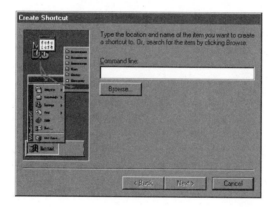

Wizards

The Windows wizards are tools that walk you through specific procedures, soliciting information so that they can take care of a lot of the grunt work for you. You don't have to use the wizards, but when you are learning Windows, they are a great way to quickly carry out tasks that might otherwise be a bit confusing. If you make a wrong selection or enter wrong information while using one of the wizards, just click the Back button to retrace your steps, correct your mistake, and then click Next to move forward again.

3. If you are an experienced DOS user, you can probably figure out what to type in the Command Line edit box (*C:\My Documents\Staff Party\Directions\East Directions.rtf,* but you must enclose the path of the document in quotation marks and include its extension; see the tip on page 35 for information about paths). Otherwise, click the Browse button to display this dialog box and look for the document:

4. With the contents of the C: drive displayed in the Look In box, double-click first the My Documents folder, then the Staff Party folder, and then the Directions folder.

5. Change the setting in the Files Of Type drop-down list box to All Files to display the Directions folder's contents.

6. Finally, double-click the East Directions document to close the Browse dialog box and enter the path of the selected document in the Command Line edit box.

7. Click Next to display this wizard dialog box:

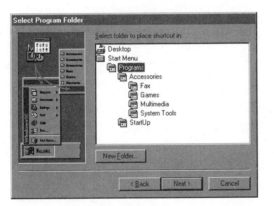

This dialog box displays all the possible locations you can select as a home for a shortcut to the specified document. Notice that Programs is the only first-level submenu of the Start menu to which you can add shortcuts.

8. With the Programs folder selected, click New Folder to create a submenu for your documents. The wizard adds a new subfolder called Program Group (1) within the Programs folder and places it in alphabetical order in the subfolder diagram.

9. Type *A Priority* as the new folder's name (we chose this name so that the new folder will be placed at the top of the list) and then click Next to display the wizard's last box, which is shown on the next page.

Selecting locations for new submenus

Using the Run command

If you are used to typing commands on a command line, you might want to use the Run command on the Start menu to quickly start programs or move directly to folders (directories) or documents. Simply type the path and name of the program or the path of the folder or document in the Open edit box of the Run dialog box and click OK. (See page 88 for more information.)

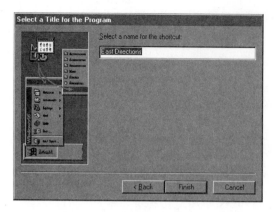

10. Click Finish and then click OK to close the Taskbar Properties dialog box.

Now for the acid test:

1. Click the Start button to display the Start menu, point to Programs, and then point to A Priority. Here's the shortcut to the document, just waiting to be clicked:

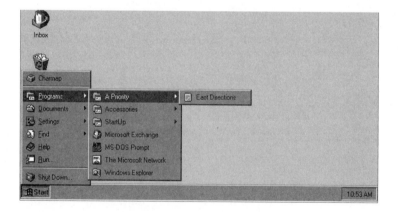

Adding Shortcuts to the StartUp Submenu

When exploring the Start menu, you may have noticed the StartUp submenu and wondered about its purpose. If you use a particular program in almost every computing session, you can have Windows automatically start that program whenever you turn on your computer. All you have to do is put a shortcut to the program in the StartUp folder. Then when you turn on your machine, Windows checks the StartUp folder and starts any programs it contains without you lifting a finger.

To demonstrate, let's put a shortcut to the Calculator program in your StartUp folder. Follow these steps:

1. Click the Start button, point to Settings, choose Taskbar to display the Taskbar Properties dialog box, and click the Start Menu Programs tab.

Adding program shortcuts to the StartUp submenu

2. Click Add to start the Create Shortcut Wizard and in the first dialog box, type *C:\Windows\Calc.exe* in the Command Line edit box and click Next.

3. In the second dialog box, select the StartUp folder at the bottom of the list box and click Next.

4. In the last dialog box, change the name in the edit box to *Calculator* and click Finish.

5. Finally, click OK to close the Taskbar Properties dialog box.

To test this StartUp shortcut, you need to restart your computer. Follow these steps:

1. Click the Start button and choose Shut Down to display the Shut Down Windows dialog box.

Restarting your computer

2. Click the Restart The Computer option and then click Yes. Windows shuts itself down, and when it restarts, you see the Calculator open on the desktop.

Removing Shortcuts from the Start Menu

You now have instant access to the Calculator through two shortcuts: the desktop icon and the shortcut on the StartUp submenu. Let's remove the shortcut from the StartUp submenu (you can use this technique to remove any Start menu shortcut):

1. Right-click a blank area of the taskbar, choose Properties, and click the Start Menu Programs tab.

2. Click the Remove button to display the dialog box shown on the next page.

3. Double-click the StartUp folder and select Calculator.

4. Click the Remove button, click Close to close the Remove Shortcuts/Folders dialog box, and then click OK to close the Taskbar Properties dialog box.

Notice that removing the shortcut from the StartUp menu has not closed the Calculator now on your screen, nor has it in any way affected the Calc program stored on your hard drive.

Multitasking

The term *multitasking* might sound intimidating, but the concept is simple: Multitasking is running more than one program at the same time. Although being able to organize documents logically and get to them quickly will undoubtedly increase your efficiency, multitasking will probably do more to boost your productivity than anything else.

Technically speaking, multitasking means carrying out two or more tasks at the same time. For example, you might be writing a report while your computer is printing another document, or your communications program is downloading information from an online service, or your e-mail program is receiving an incoming message. In practice, most people don't often multitask in the true sense of the word. They are more likely to open two or three programs and work with one while the others sit idly in memory, waiting until they are needed. The programs have been started and they are readily available, but they aren't actually doing any work.

Having several programs open at once saves you time by allowing you to keep all the information you need at your fingertips, whether it is stored in a report, a spreadsheet, a database, or any other type of document. If you're in the middle of writing a letter and need to look up some figures in a spreadsheet, you no longer have to stop what you are doing, quit the word processor, load the spreadsheet, find the figures, and then start your word processor again. You can simply flip between windows to get the information you need.

Foreground vs. Background

Although you can have more than one program running at the same time, only one program can run *in the foreground*, meaning that its window is active and receiving input from you. Any other open programs run *in the background*, meaning that they are behind the scenes, either carrying out some prescribed task or waiting for your next instruction. To see the difference between a foreground and a background program, follow these steps:

Running in the foreground

Running in the background

1. With Calculator open, click the Start button, point to Programs, point to Accessories, and click WordPad to open a new document in a WordPad window.

Multitasking with windows

2. If the window is maximized, click its Restore button to shrink the window, and then move it down (drag its title bar) so that you can see the Calculator's display bar in the background.

3. Type *4*. Because the WordPad window is in the foreground, the 4 is inserted at the top of the new WordPad document.

4. Click anywhere in the Calculator window to bring it to the foreground and make it active, and then type *4* again. The 4 appears in the Calculator's display bar.

5. Click the WordPad window to bring it to the foreground, and type another *4*, which is inserted in the document.

6. Click the Calculator window and type yet another *4*, which appears in the Calculator's display bar. The results are shown on the next page.

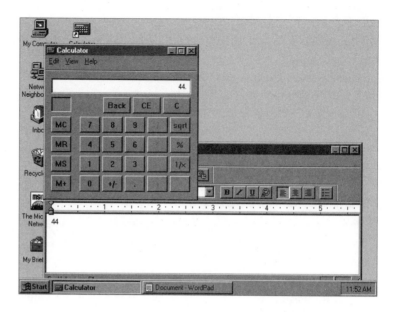

Switching Among Running Programs

You have just seen how easy it is to switch to a program when you can see part of its window. If you are working in a maximized window and can't see the windows of programs running in the background, you use the taskbar buttons to switch to other open programs. As a demonstration, suppose you are responsible for providing appetizers for the staff party, and while browsing through the Yellow Pages, you use WordPad to take down information about potential caterers. Follow these steps:

1. Activate the WordPad window, maximize it, and delete the 4s.

2. Type *Fill Your Belly Deli* and press Enter.

3. Type *555-1001*, and press Enter twice.

4. Add these delis to the list:

   Katz's Northwest-Style Deli
   555-5364
   (Press Enter twice)

   The Pickle Barrel
   555-9292
   (Press Enter)

The WordPad window looks like this:

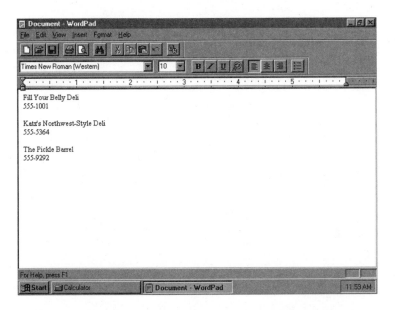

5. Now save the document. Choose Save As from the File menu, use the Save In drop-down list box and the folder window below to specify the Staff Party folder as the storage location, enter *Caterers* as the name, select Rich Text Format (RTF) as the Save As Type setting, and click Save.

Suppose you are using your handy list to call the companies and get estimates. The first deli quotes you a per-person price of $6.25 for a regular assortment of appetizers and $7.75 for a deluxe assortment. You want to calculate the respective costs for 72 people. This is a job for the Calculator. Try the following:

1. Click the Calculator button on the taskbar to display the Calculator window.

Multitasking with the taskbar

2. Click the C (for *Clear*) button to clear the display bar. Then click the buttons for 72, click *, click the buttons for 6.25, and click =. The display bar shows the total, 450.

3. Now you need to go back to the Caterers document to record the cost of the regular appetizers. Click the WordPad button

on the taskbar to display its window. The Calculator window
is once again obscured by the WordPad window.

4. Click at the beginning of the blank line after the first caterer's
telephone number to position the insertion point there, type
Regular: $450, and press Enter.

Here's another way to switch between open programs:

Multitasking with Alt+Tab

1. Hold down the Alt key and without releasing the key, press
the Tab key. A window appears in the middle of the screen
in which the open programs are represented by icons. A box
indicates the program Windows will switch to when you
release Alt.

2. Still holding down the Alt key, press Tab again. The box
moves to the icon of the other open program. Press Tab again
and then release the Alt key. Windows displays the Calculator's window.

3. Click C, click the buttons for 72, click *, click the buttons for
7.75, and then click =. The display bar shows the total, 558.

4. Hold down Alt and press Tab to switch back to WordPad, and
with the insertion point at the beginning of the blank line after
the regular cost, type *Deluxe: $558*, and press Enter.

Arranging Windows

If you have only a couple of programs open and you want to
be able to see them both at the same time, you can easily size
and arrange their windows manually. If you have several
programs open, it is quicker to let Windows arrange them for
you. Try this:

Cascading windows

1. Right-click a blank area of the taskbar and choose Cascade
from the object menu to arrange the Calculator and WordPad
windows like this:

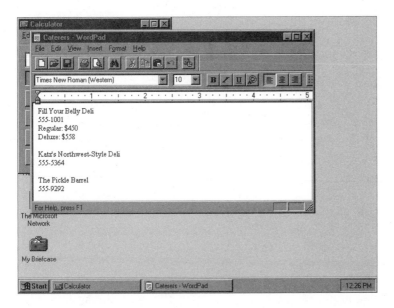

As you can see, choosing Cascade causes all open windows to overlap so that the title bar of each window is visible.

2. Now right-click the taskbar and choose Tile Vertically from the object menu to arrange the windows like this:

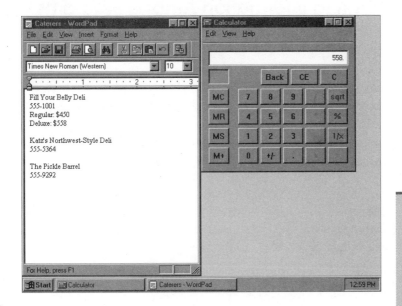

Selective arrangements

The Cascade and Tile commands ignore minimized windows, so if you want, for example, to arrange only two of the five windows that you have open, minimize the three you don't want to see and then choose the appropriate command from the taskbar object menu.

Tiling windows

The Tile Vertically and Tile Horizontally commands arrange and size the windows so that none of them overlap. (Some windows, like the Calculator window, cannot be resized. As a result, the Tile and Cascade commands cannot arrange them as neatly as other windows.)

Now suppose the second deli has quoted you a per-person price of $5.75 for a regular assortment of appetizers and $7.25 for a deluxe assortment. Follow these steps to calculate the costs:

1. Click the Calculator window, click C, click the buttons for 72, click *, click the buttons for 5.75, and click =. The display bar shows the total, 414.

2. Click the Caterers window, click an insertion point at the beginning of the blank line after the second caterer's telephone number, type *Regular: $414*, and press Enter.

3. Repeat steps 1 and 2 to calculate the second caterer's deluxe appetizer cost and enter it in the document.

Sharing Information Among Programs

Windows 95 makes it easier than ever before to use the information from one program in another program. Need a logo for your letterhead? You can create one with a paint program, copy it to the Clipboard, and paste it into a word-processing document, in three easy steps. Because Windows allows you to run the paint program and the word-processing program simultaneously, moving from one program to the other is a simple matter of clicking the mouse button.

To demonstrate how to transfer information, we'll use Word-Pad, Calculator, and Character Map. First we'll complete the information for the third caterer, and then we'll add a fourth. Here are the steps:

Sharing information via the Clipboard

1. Click the Calculator window, click C, click the buttons for 72, click *, click the 6 button, and click =. The display bar shows the regular appetizer cost at $6 per person, 432.

2. Choose Copy from the Calculator's Edit menu to copy the value in the display bar to the Clipboard.

3. Click the Caterers window, click an insertion point at the beginning of the blank line after the third caterer's telephone number, and type *Regular:* followed by a space.

4. Choose Paste from WordPad's Edit menu to paste the total from the Calculator into the document. Then add a dollar sign and press Enter.

5. Repeat steps 1 through 4 to calculate the third caterer's deluxe appetizer cost at $7.50 per person and paste it into the document. Here are the results:

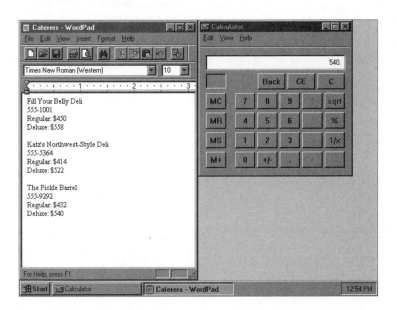

To give you more practice, we'll show you how to use Character Map, which you added to the top of the Start menu earlier in the chapter. We're going to add an entry for a deli called La Crème Fraîche (which means *Fresh Cream*) to the list. Follow these steps:

1. With the Caterer's window active, click an insertion point at the beginning of the blank line below the third caterer, press Enter, and type *La Cr*.

Dragging information

With many commercial Windows programs, you can copy information from one open program window to another by selecting the information and dragging it. This direct transfer method bypasses the Clipboard entirely.

Using Character Map →

2. Click the Start button and choose Charmap from the Start menu to display this window:

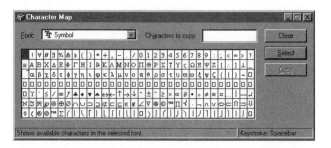

As you can see, the program displays all the characters available in the font specified in the Font box.

3. Click the arrow at the right end of the Font box and select Times New Roman from the drop-down list. The characters in the grid below change to reflect those available in that font.

Inserting special characters →

4. Check that the Characters To Copy box is empty (if it's not, delete any existing entries), click the *è* in the last row and click the Select button. The program enters the *è* in the Characters To Copy box, and the window now looks like this:

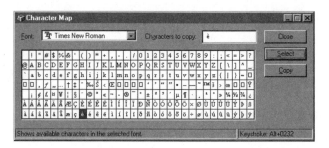

5. Click the Copy button to copy the character to the Clipboard.

6. Click the WordPad button on the taskbar to display the Caterers document and click the Paste button on the toolbar. The character appears at the insertion point.

The Paste button →

The font size of the *è* is 12 point, but the font size of the rest of the Caterers document is 10 point. Here's how to fix the problem:

1. Select the *è*, or if you have trouble selecting a single character with the mouse select the entire line.

2. Click the arrow at the right end of the Font Size box on the Formatting toolbar to drop down a list of sizes, and click 10.

Now let's complete the name of the fourth caterer:

1. Type *me Fra* and click the Character Map button on the taskbar to display its window.

2. Double-click the entry in the Characters To Copy box and press Backspace to delete it.

3. Click *î* in the last row, click the Select button, click Copy, and then click the Close button to quit Character Map.

4. Activate the WordPad window, click the Paste button to paste in the character, and finish the name by typing *che*, changing the font size to 10, and pressing Enter. Here are the results:

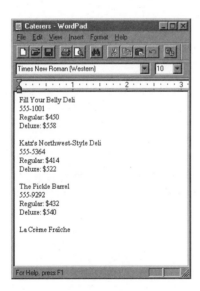

5. Type *555-6198* as the telephone number.

The last item you copied, *î*, is still on the Clipboard and stays there until it is replaced by the next item you cut or copy, or until you quit Windows. Let's sidetrack here to see the copied item on the Clipboard by following the steps on the next page.

Entering with the keyboard

In the bottom right corner of the Character Map window is the shortcut for entering the selected character from the keyboard rather than by copying and pasting it. For example, you can type the *è* character without switching to Character Map by holding down the Alt key and pressing 0, 2, 3, and 2 keys on your keyboard's numeric keypad. (You can't use the number keys across the top of your keyboard.)

Viewing the Clipboard's
contents

1. Click the Start button, point to Programs, point to Accessories, and click Clipboard Viewer to open the Clipboard window, which contains the character you just copied:

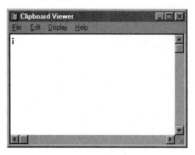

   If you don't see the Clipboard Viewer on your Accessories submenu, you will have to load it. See page 118 for instructions on how to load Windows components.

2. Right-click the taskbar and choose Tile Vertically so that you can see the Clipboard Viewer, the Caterers document, and the Calculator all at once.

3. Calculate the cost of regular appetizers at $6.50 per person and copy and paste the result in the Caterers document, noticing that the copied item replaces the existing item in the Clipboard Viewer window, like this:

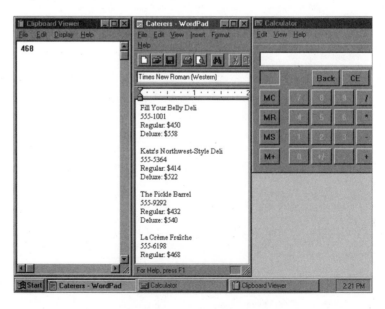

4. Repeat step 3 to calculate the cost of deluxe appetizers at $8 per person and paste the result in the Caterers document.

5. Save the document, and then close the Clipboard Viewer by clicking its Close button.

Embedding and Linking Information

If you have followed along with the examples we've covered so far, you know that sharing information among programs is easy. Just select the information in the document from which you're copying, choose Copy from the File menu, open the document in which you want to paste the information, select an insertion point, and choose Paste from the File menu.

However, the power of Windows far exceeds this simple kind of copying and pasting. With Windows, you can create a document that is a patchwork of pieces created in the different programs. This kind of sharing means that you can maintain information in separate documents formatted for use by the program that created them, but you can also use that information in documents created by other programs.

These "patchwork" documents are made possible by a feature called *OLE* (pronounced *olay*). The technology behind OLE is pretty complicated, but you don't have to be an OLE expert to take advantage of it. Here is a quick overview of the concept so that you can decide when and how to use it.

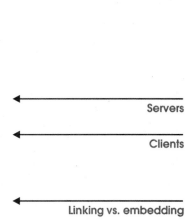

OLE

The *O* in OLE stands for *object.* As you know, an object is an item or an element of a document. It can be a block of text, a graphic, a table, a chart, and so on. The program that creates the object is called the *server,* and the original document is called the *source document.* The object can be used by another program called the *client*, and the client document in which the object is used is sometimes called the *container document.*

Servers

Clients

To create a patchwork document, you can *link* an object to the document (the *L* in OLE) or you can *embed* the object (the *E*). When you link information that is stored in a source document to a container document, you need both the source document and the container document in order to be able to

Linking vs. embedding

display the object. When you embed information, the information becomes part of the container document and you no longer need the source document.

So how does all this influence how you go about creating patchwork documents? If the object you want to use in a patchwork document is likely to change and you want to be sure that every instance of the object in every document where the information is used reflects the changes, it is best to create the information in its own source document and then link the object where it's needed. If the information is not going to change, embedding might be the best way to go because embedded information can be edited in the container document without the source document having to be present. Bear in mind, however, that documents that contain embedded objects can get very large.

So that's the scoop on OLE. Now let's see how you might go about using it. In the following examples, we'll use the Paint program that comes with Windows to create a graphic. Then we'll use the graphic in four documents. Here we go:

Using Paint

1. Close all open windows and then start Paint, which is located on the Accessories submenu.

2. Use the Pencil and Text tools to create a simple map like this:

OLE-supporting programs

Most recent versions of commercial Windows programs support OLE in some fashion, but not all are capable of acting both as an OLE server and an OLE client, and not all support the most recent incarnation of the OLE technology. If you are working with an older version of a favorite program, you will need to experiment to find out what its capabilities are.

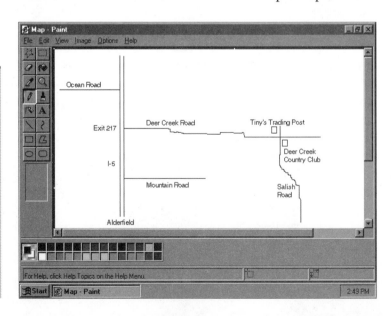

You can hold down the Shift key while dragging the Pencil tool to draw straight lines. If you don't know how to work with the Text tool, don't worry about including the street names. The goal here is not to teach you how to use Paint (you can experiment on your own) but to demonstrate OLE.

3. Choose Save As from the File menu and save the graphic with the name *Map* in the Directions folder where you have stored your Directions documents.

4. Close the Paint window.

Now we'll embed the graphic in a Directions document:

1. Open the North Directions document (maximize the Word-Pad window if necessary), hold down Ctrl and press End to move to the end of the document, press Enter a couple of times, type *Here is a map:*, and press Enter twice.

2. Choose Object from the Insert menu to display the dialog box shown here:

Embedding objects

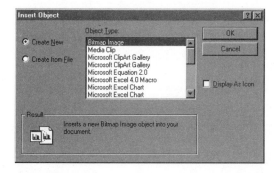

3. With Bitmap Image selected in the Object Type list box, select the Create From File option and when the dialog box changes to let you enter the name of the document, click the Browse button to display the dialog box shown earlier on page 64.

4. Locate the Map document, double-click it to return to the Insert Object dialog box with the document's address in the File edit box, and click OK. The dialog box closes, and you return to the North Directions document, where the map has been embedded in a large frame.

Other programs

Although the instructions given here are specific to WordPad, the procedure is very similar for other Windows programs that support OLE. To link or embed an object in another program, look for an Object or Insert Object command and follow the directions given in the dialog box, using Help if necessary. (Some programs also forge links by means of a Paste Special command on the Edit menu.)

5. Scroll upward to see the map in place:

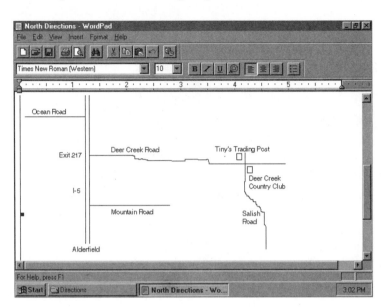

6. Save the document.

Now suppose you need to change Ocean Road in the map to Ocean Avenue. Instead of making the change in Paint and re-embedding the object in North Directions, you can change it using Paint's tools without leaving WordPad, like this:

1. Double-click the map object. The screen looks as shown here:

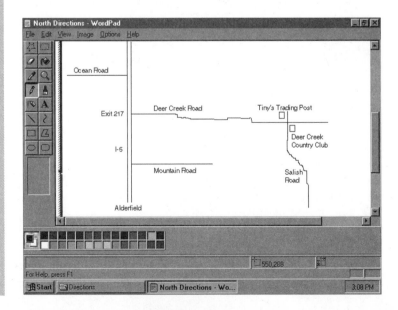

Creating new objects

When you choose Object from the Insert menu, you have the option of creating a new object of the specified type. For example, if the Map document did not already exist, clicking OK in the Insert Object dialog box with the Create New option and Bitmap Image selected would display a frame in the open North Directions document, and Paint's menus and tools would appear. You could then draw the map object directly in the frame. Clicking outside the frame would remove Paint's menus and tools but leave the map object in place as part of the document. You could edit the map later by simply double-clicking it to redisplay Paint's menus and tools.

As you can see, the menu bar has changed, and the window has many of the characteristics of a Paint window, even though the title bar shows that you are still in WordPad.

2. If you know how to use the Eraser and Text tools, make the necessary changes. (If you don't, use the Pencil tool to make a squiggle. You just need to see that when you embed an object, you can change it using the program that created it, even though the object is now stored in another document.)

3. Save the document and then close it.

Instead of embedding the map as a graphic object, you can embed it as an icon. Follow these steps to see the difference:

1. Open the South Directions document, hold down Ctrl and press End to move to the end of the document, press Enter a couple of times, type *Double-click the icon below if you want to see a map:*, and press Enter twice.

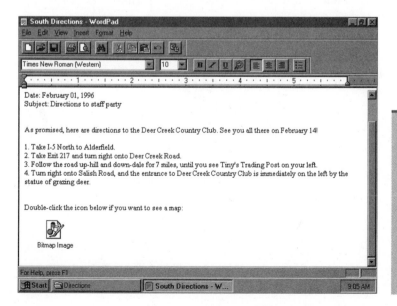

Embedding objects as icons

2. Choose Object from the Insert menu and with Bitmap Image selected as the object type, select the Create From File option.

3. Use the Browse dialog box to locate the Map document, double-click it to return to the Insert Object dialog box with the document's address in the File edit box, select the Display As Icon option, and click OK. Here's the result:

Editing embedded objects

When you make changes to an embedded object (one that is not linked to its source document), you are changing the version of the object that is stored in the open container document. Your changes do not in any way affect the original source document.

4. Save the document and then double-click the icon. A Paint window opens displaying nothing but the map, as shown here (we've maximized the window):

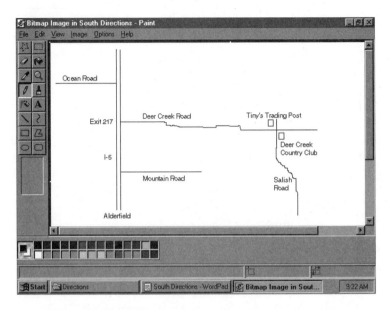

Notice that the original Map document was not affected by the changes you made on page 83. (See the tip on page 83.)

5. Make any changes you want in this window, and then choose the Exit & Return To South Directions command from the File menu to close the window and return to your document.

6. Close the South Directions document.

Now let's link the map to two different documents, first as a graphic object and then as an icon:

Linking objects

1. Open the East Directions document, hold down Ctrl and press End to move to the end of the document, press Enter a couple of times, type *Here is a map:*, and press Enter twice.

2. Choose Object from the Insert menu and with Bitmap Image selected in the Object Type list box, select the Create From File option.

3. Use the Browse dialog box to locate the Map document, double-click it to return to the Insert Object dialog box with

the document's address in the File edit box, select the Link option, and click OK.

4. Scroll upward to see the map in place. It looks exactly as the embedded object did in the North Directions document.

5. Save the document.

6. Open the West Directions document, hold down Ctrl and press End to move to the end of the document, press Enter a couple of times, type *Double-click the icon below if you want to see a map:*, and press Enter twice.

Linking objects as icons

7. Choose Object from the Insert menu and with Bitmap Image selected as the Object Type, select Create From File.

8. Use the Browse dialog box to locate the Map document, double-click it to return to the Insert Object dialog box with the document's address in the File edit box, select the Link and Display As Icon options, and click OK. The West Directions document now looks the same as the South Directions document.

9. Save the document and close any open WordPad windows.

   Now suppose once again that Ocean Road should be Ocean Avenue. Because the object is linked to the source Paint document, you can edit the map in Paint and the change will be reflected in the two linked documents. Follow these steps:

1. Double-click the Map document icon in the Directions folder to open the map in Paint. Use the Eraser and Text tools to make the necessary changes. (Or make a squiggle or two with the Pencil tool.)

Editing source documents for linked objects

2. Save the map.

3. Open the East Directions document and scroll the window. Refer to the image on the next page to see how the linked object faithfully reflects the changes you made to the Paint document.

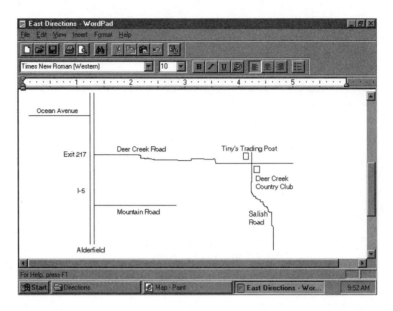

4. Now open the West Directions document and double-click the Map icon. You move to a Paint window with the new version of the map displayed.

5. Tidy up the desktop by closing all open windows.

Depending on the programs you are using, you will find that OLE sometimes doesn't work quite as well as you would like. Or you will find that it works well under certain circumstances, such as when the source document is open, and not so well under others, such as when the source document is closed. This technology is evolving, and Windows programs have implemented it to varying degrees. But if you need to create dynamic documents that contain objects from different programs, it is worth taking the time to experiment with OLE so that you understand how it works in the particular programs you use.

Using DOS Programs

If you've been working with computers for a while, you may have a favorite DOS program that you want to use under Windows 95. You'll be happy to know that Windows 95 makes it fairly easy to start and use DOS programs, and even lets you run Windows and DOS programs simultaneously.

Starting in DOS mode

If you know that you are going to be using only DOS programs in a particular work session, you can turn on your computer, wait for *Starting Windows 95* to appear on the screen, immediately press the F8 key, and then select Command Prompt Only from the list of options. Simply turn off the computer at the C:\> prompt when you're finished.

If you want to be able to start a DOS program from the Start menu but it is not listed there, you can add it to the Start menu or to the Programs submenu just like any Windows program (see page 63). You can also double-click the program in a folder window or the Windows Explorer window to start it. In addition, you have two other options:

Starting DOS programs

- You can choose Run from the Start menu to display the dialog box shown here:

Using the Run command

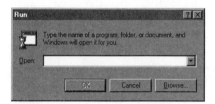

You then enter the path and name of the program in the Open edit box or use the Browse dialog box to locate the file. Then click OK to start the program. (You can also use the Run command to open a folder or document.) When you have finished, you quit the program in the usual way and return to Windows.

For example, suppose you want to run the ZPARK program to "park" your hard drive so that its read/write heads won't jiggle around while you move your computer. You choose Run from the Start menu, use the Browse dialog box to find ZPARK in a Utilities folder where you keep favorite little programs like this one, and click OK to start the program. When ZPARK finishes, press any key to return to DOS and then close the ZPARK window.

- You can choose MS-DOS Prompt from the Programs submenu of the Start menu to load the Windows version of DOS. You can then enter the path and name of the program at the C:\> prompt, just as you would in DOS. (This is the preferred method of running the program when you need to give information on the command line in addition to the name of the program.) When you have finished your work with the program, you exit it as usual. Back at the C:\> prompt, you quit MS-DOS Prompt by typing *exit*.

Using the MS-DOS Prompt command

For example, say you want to use the PKZIP file-compression program to compress a directory of letters to clients so that you can squeeze them onto a floppy disk. Double-clicking PKZIP's filename in a folder window or using the Run command simply displays a list of the information you need to supply when you start the program. So you choose MS-DOS Prompt from the Programs submenu, change to the directory where the letters are stored, type *pkzip letters.zip *.** at the C:\> prompt, and press Enter to tell PKZIP to compress all the files in the directory into one file called LETTERS.ZIP. When PKZIP has finished its task, you type *exit* to quit MS-DOS Prompt and return to Windows.

Running DOS programs full-screen or in windows

You can run most, but not all, DOS programs either full-screen or in their own windows. To display a DOS program that is running full-screen in a window, hold down Alt and press Enter. Press Alt+Enter again to switch back to full-screen. Full-screen DOS programs completely take over the screen and don't have to give up space to such items as a title bar or status bar. Windowed DOS programs gain some of the functionality of Windows programs, including the ability to copy and paste data between programs. (See page 74 for more information, but bear in mind that sharing information with a DOS program can be more complicated than sharing with

Restarting in DOS mode

If you have been working in Windows and you want to use only DOS programs for the remainder of the work session, choose Shut Down from the Start menu, select the Restart The Computer In MS-DOS Mode option, and click Yes. At the end of the DOS session, check that the C:\> prompt is on your screen and turn off the computer.

Repeating the Run command

The entry in the Open edit box of the Run dialog box is retained from one session to the next, so if you frequently use this method to start a particular program or open a folder or document, you don't have to enter the program, folder, or document from scratch each time. The Open drop-down list displays your most recent entries; to repeat the Run command for a recently used program, folder, or document, simply select the correct path and name from the list and click OK.

another Windows program. You will have to experiment with your own DOS programs to see how well copying and pasting works.)

When you have finished working in a DOS program, you should quit the program just as you used to when you were working in DOS. It's tempting to simply click the Close button of a windowed program, but quitting in the usual way minimizes the risk of any problems. If a program that has finished running remains on the screen with the word *Finished* in the title bar, you can close its window by clicking its Close button. When you shut down Windows, it will automatically close any open Windows programs but will ask you to manually close any open DOS programs.

Closing DOS programs

Solving Common Problems 4

We discuss how to reduce potential problems to mild inconveniences by planning ahead. Included are discussions of safeguarding files with Backup, optimizing disks with ScanDisk and Disk Defragmenter, and creating more storage space with DriveSpace.

Create more storage space on your hard disk or a floppy disk

Clean up a fragmented hard disk with Disk Defragmenter

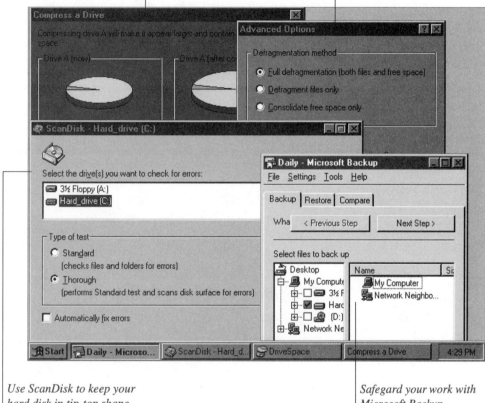

Use ScanDisk to keep your hard disk in tip-top shape

Safegard your work with Microsoft Backup

I n this chapter, we show you how to use some of the problem-solving tools that come with Windows 95. As you work your way through our examples, your goal is two-fold: First, you want to prevent problems to the extent possible; and second, you want to have a strategy in place for dealing with the problems that will inevitably occur. How well-prepared you are for these problems could make the difference between a minor inconvenience and a major catastrophe.

Many people have an aversion to thinking about problems before they happen. Others take Murphy's Law ("anything that can go wrong will go wrong") quite literally and build contingency plans into every undertaking. Between the optimists and the pessimists, the rest of us hope for the best and learn from experience. Unfortunately, learning from experience can be very painful (and expensive) where computers are concerned. Take our word for it: If you have important documents that would be difficult or time-consuming to reconstruct, a little time spent planning ahead will pay big dividends in the event of software or hardware misbehavior.

Creating a Startup Disk

A startup disk is a floppy disk you can use to start ("boot") your computer if for some reason it decides to play dead. The disk contains the files you would need in the event of a crash, such as:

- The operating system files needed to start your computer (these are hidden files; see page 38)

- Various programs you might need to track down problems or recover files, including ScanDisk (see page 103)

A startup disk might have been created for your computer when Windows 95 was installed on your machine. If for some reason you don't have that startup disk, you can create one now by following these steps:

1. Click the Start button and choose Settings and then Control Panel from the Start menu.

2. Double-click the Add/Remove Programs icon and click the Startup Disk tab to display this dialog box:

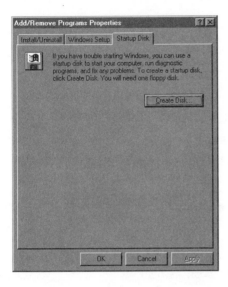

3. Click the Create Disk button and then follow the prompts, inserting your Windows 95 installation disks or CD-ROM and a floppy disk when requested.

4. Click OK to close the dialog box.

Now if your computer plays dead some morning, you can use the startup disk to start Windows 95 (see the adjacent tip).

Safeguarding Your Documents

An effective plan for safeguarding your documents has two phases: First, and most obvious, take steps to avoid losing them, and second, back them up regularly so that they are easy to recover if you do make a mistake.

General File-Safety Strategies

If you keep the following pointers in mind, you may never have to deal with lost documents:

- Windows sometimes displays a confirmation prompt when it wants you to think twice about a particular action. You should

---

Using the startup disk

If you turn on your computer one day and it refuses to get going, turn it off again, insert the startup disk in the A: drive, and flip the switch. Your computer uses the files on the disk to start itself, and you then see *A:\>* on your screen. Former DOS users will recognize this cryptic symbol as the command prompt, meaning that the computer is waiting for you to type a command. Type *C:* and press Enter. Then type *win* to start Windows. If your computer's reluctance to start was only temporary, you can then get to work. If the problem persists and you know what you're doing, you can sleuth around and try to identify and fix the problem. If you don't, get an expert to help you.

take these prompts seriously. It's easy to get in the habit of hitting Enter without really reading them.

Delete to the Recycle Bin ➝ • Delete documents to the Recycle Bin so that you can easily undelete them.

Organize folders and documents ➝ • Keep your folders and documents organized (see Chapter 2). As a general rule, don't keep copies of the same document in several different folders. If you work on one version of a document one day and on another version another day, you'll lose one set of changes. No program we know of can help you merge the changes so that they are all in one document.

Save often ➝ • The most important way of safeguarding your documents is the easiest: Save your work often.

Following these tips will certainly keep the chances of losing documents to a minimum. But to reduce the impact of the rare mishap, nothing works as well as backing up your files, so we'll discuss that next.

Backing Up

Backing up is like flossing your teeth or taking out the garbage: necessary, but not very exciting. It's easy to put it off. But we can't stress the point enough: Sooner or later, something will go wrong, and you will lose valuable documents. Just as a bad dental checkup can induce people to start flossing, losing documents can, overnight, instill the habit of backing up.

The term *backing up* simply means making a copy of your documents that will be available in case you have problems with your computer. Storing copies safely off your computer can reduce disasters to mere inconveniences and make recovering your work a matter of simply transfering the copies from floppy disks or tape. Taking some time to evaluate your needs and develop a simple and effective backup strategy can really pay off when the inevitable document loss occurs.

You can use floppy disks, a tape drive, a removable hard drive, or another computer as the storage medium for backups. For purposes of this discussion, we assume you are backing up to floppy disks. Windows provides two methods for backing up documents: copying them and using Microsoft Backup. Which method you use depends primarily on the number of documents to be backed up.

- The simplest strategy for backing up just a few documents is to copy them using the techniques discussed on page 50.

Backing up a few documents

- If you get to the point where you are backing up large numbers of documents or single documents that are larger than one disk, you will probably want to use Microsoft Backup, which employs a special coding system to compress files as it copies them so that they take up less space. You must then use the Restore component of Backup to restore the files back onto your hard disk in a usable format.

Backing up many documents

Deciding on a Backup Strategy

Before you take a look at Microsoft Backup, you need to work out a backup system and schedule. Many factors will influence the system you develop, including how often your documents change and how much damage would result if you lost, say, a day's work. As an example, suppose you analyze your work habits and decide the following:

- Of the programs you use regularly, all but one (a page-layout program with many customized settings) could easily be reinstalled from their original disks if your computer crashed. The page-layout program should be backed up once a week to avoid you having to reset all its options.

- You keep all your documents, no matter which program you use to create them, in the My Documents folder on your C: drive. These documents change constantly, as you update existing documents, create new ones, and delete old ones. They should be backed up daily.

Here is an example of a pretty rigorous backup system that meets these needs:

- You set aside four disks, or sets of disks, labeled *Monday*, *Tuesday*, *Wednesday*, and *Thursday*. You also set aside a fifth disk, or set of disks, labeled *End of Week*.

A sample backup strategy

- At the end of each of the first four days of the week, you back up the folders and documents in the My Documents folder on that day's disk(s). For this daily procedure, you do an incremental backup, which speeds up the backup process (see page 99 for more information).

- At the end of each week, you back up all the folders and documents in My Documents and the page-layout program on the End of Week disk(s). For this weekly procedure, you do a full backup (again, see page 99).

- The cycle starts over at the beginning of the next week.

You can modify this backup system in many ways to meet your individual needs. For example, you might want to start by making a backup of the entire contents of your hard disk (a full system backup) that you can store away from your office to safeguard your data against fire or vandalism.

Using Microsoft Backup

The new Microsoft Backup program is faster, more powerful, and easier to use than previous versions. To experiment with Backup, you need to have a floppy disk handy. (You can use the disk you formatted in Chapter 2 or any other disk containing information you don't need.) Then follow these steps:

1. Click the Start button, point to Programs, point to Accessories, point to System Tools, and click Backup. (If Backup isn't on the System Tools submenu, it is probably not installed on your computer. To install the program, follow the instructions for adding a Windows component on page 118. Backup can be found under Disk Tools in the Components list.)

2. When Backup's welcome window appears, click OK to close it. Backup then displays a message box telling you about the full system backup file set. (See the tip on page 99 for more information.) Click OK to close the message box.

3. Depending on whether or not you have a tape drive, Backup then displays another message box. Read the message and click OK. You should see a Microsoft Backup window similar to this one:

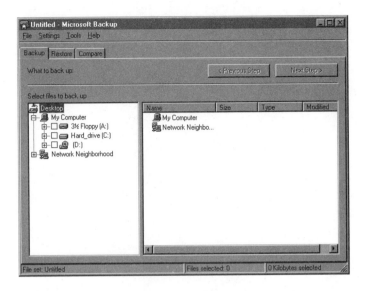

As you can see, the Backup tab of the Microsoft Backup window looks very similar to the Windows Explorer window, and you display folder contents in the left and right panes the same way you do in Windows Explorer (see page 40).

4. Click the C: drive icon in the left pane to display its contents in the right pane.

5. Click the check box beside the My Documents folder in the right pane to indicate that you want to back up all the documents in this folder. The window now looks like this:

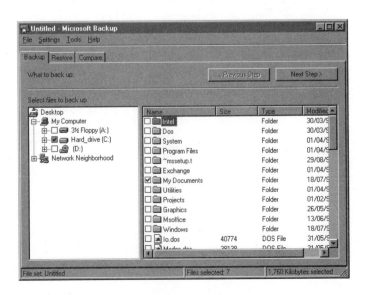

Comparing backed up files

To ensure that backup files exactly match the originals, you can choose Options from the Settings menu, select the Verify Backup Data Automatically option on the Backup tab, and click OK. However, the backup operation then takes a bit longer. As an alternative, you can back up your files, click the Compare tab of the Microsoft Backup window, specify which files you want to compare, and click the Start Compare button. Backup then reports any differences between the original and backup files.

Specifying a backup
destination

6. Click the Next Step button to display this window, where you specify where to make the backup:

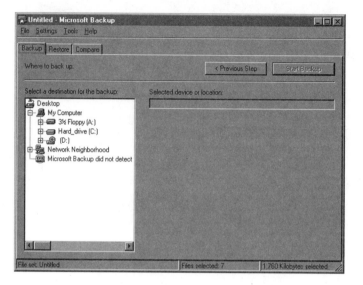

7. Click the floppy drive icon.

8. Now you need to select the type of backup you want. Choose Options from the Settings menu and then click the Backup tab to display these options:

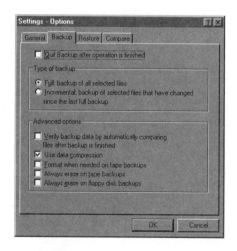

9. As you can see, you can select either Full or Incremental as the Type Of Backup option. Select Full to back up all the selected files, and select Incremental to back up only the

Using filters

Suppose one of your project folders contains 20 documents that you are actively working on. The program associated with those documents retains the previous versions of the files every time you save them by appending a hidden BAK extension to the filenames. When you back up your work using Microsoft Backup, you want to safeguard the current documents but you don't want to take up space with all the BAK files. To exclude them from the backup operation, start Microsoft Backup, choose File Filtering from the Settings menu, select BAK File from the File Types list box, click Exclude, and then click OK. When you return to the Microsoft Backup window, select the project folder whose files you want to back up. Even though the entire folder is selected, the BAK files will not be backed up. (You can also exclude files whose dates fall within a specified range.)

selected files that have changed since they were last backed up. Because you have not yet backed up the selected files, click OK to accept the default Full option.

10. Back in the Microsoft Backup window, click Start Backup.

11. When the Backup Set Label dialog box appears, type today's date, beginning with the actual day of the week (for example, type *Monday, 2-5-96*; slashes aren't allowed), and click OK. Backup prompts you to insert a disk and goes to work, seeking out and backing up the selected files and displaying its progress on the screen as it goes. If you were backing up a large group of files, Backup would prompt you each time it needed you to insert a new disk.

12. When you see the *Operation complete* message, click OK. Backup then reports how many files and bytes it backed up, how long the backup operation took, and the extent to which it compressed the files. After reading the information, press Enter to return to the Microsoft Backup window.

Creating File Sets

When you backed up the My Documents folder, you had to select the folder and select the backup location before Backup could do its job. You can greatly streamline your backup operations by creating file sets that will take care of the selection part of the process for you. A file set tells Backup what to back up and how. As an example, let's save a file set for an incremental backup of the My Documents folder:

1. On the Backup tab of the Microsoft Backup window, display the contents of the C: drive, select the My Documents folder, and click Next Step.

2. Next, select your floppy drive as the backup medium.

3. Choose Options from the Settings menu, select Incremental on the Backup tab, and click OK.

4. Choose Save As from the File menu, type *Daily* as the file set name, and click Save.

Full system backup file set

By default, Microsoft Backup creates a full system backup file set the first time you use the Backup program. This file set contains all the files on your hard drive, including all the registry files which your computer needs in order to work properly. It's a good idea to copy the full system backup file set to a safe place (such as a tape or floppy disk) so that, in the event of a catastrophe, you can restore your entire hard drive. To copy the full system backup file set, first locate it on your hard drive in the Accessories subfolder of the Program Files folder and then copy it in the usual manner. (See page 50 if you need help copying files.) If you and your computer are faced with a catastrophe, you can then restore your hard drive by using the Restore tab of the Microsoft Backup window. (See page 101 for more information about restoring files.) To make sure your full system backup file set is current, you must also back it up on a regular basis. The easiest way to back up this file set is to open the Accessories window and then drag the Full System Backup icon to the Backup icon.

Backup saves your document selections and Options dialog-box settings in the file set. Now you can reduce the steps required to carry out that particular backup operation by simply opening the file set. Follow these steps:

Backing up file sets ──▶ 1. On the Backup tab of the Microsoft Backup window, choose Open File Set from the File menu to display this dialog box:

2. Select Daily from the list and click Open. The window changes to look like this:

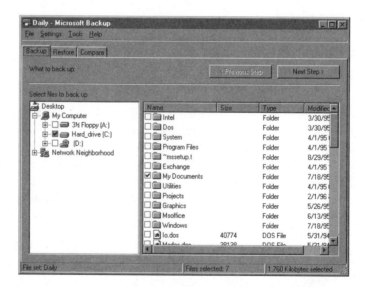

Adjusting file sets

If you want to back up a set of files that is almost, but not quite, the same as one specified by a file set you have already created, you can use the Open File Set command on the File menu to open the file set and then adjust the selections in the Backup window to tailor the file set for this particular backup operation. Unless you save the new definition, the file set will revert to its original settings the next time you use it.

In the left pane, the C: drive check box is gray with a check mark to indicate that part of this drive will be backed up. In the right pane, the My Documents check box is white with a check mark to indicate that the entire folder will be backed up.

3. Choose Options from the Settings menu and click the Backup tab, where Incremental is selected as the Type Of Backup option. Click Cancel.

To back up the folder, you would click Next Step, select the floppy drive, click Start Backup, and enter a backup set label.

Restoring Documents

If Murphy's Law proves correct, you will at some point need to restore files from disk. Let's give the restoration process a dry run. For the next example, you need to simulate the accidental deletion of the documents from your My Documents folder by changing the name of the folder, like this:

1. Open My Computer (drag the Microsoft Backup window out of the way if necessary) and display the C: drive window.

2. Right-click the My Documents folder, choose Rename from the object menu, type *Old Documents*, and press Enter.

3. Close the open folder windows.

Now the My Documents folder is "gone." Let's restore it and its contents from the backup disk you just created:

1. With the Microsoft Backup window open on your screen, click the Restore tab to display this window:

← Restoring from floppy disk

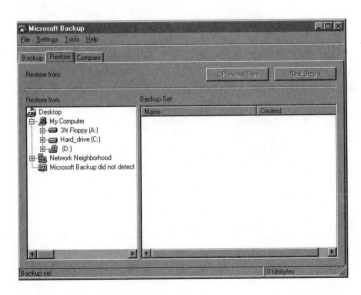

The left pane displays possible locations of backup files.

2. Insert the backup disk you created earlier in your floppy drive, select the floppy drive in the left pane, and click Next Step. You see this window:

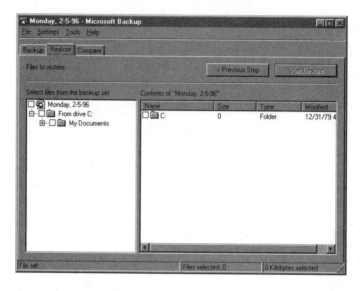

3. Select My Documents in the left pane and click the Start Restore button. (You can selectively restore folders and documents by selecting them in both the left and right panes.)

4. Once the files are restored, click the Close button to close the Microsoft Backup window, and then remove the disk from your floppy drive.

5. In My Computer, open the C: drive window, which now displays an Old Documents folder and a My Documents folder.

6. Close all open windows.

From this simple demonstration, you can see how easily you can recover files in the event of a catastrophe, but only if you have taken the time to back up your documents.

Optimizing Your Hard Disk

The risk of experiencing disk and file problems is greatly reduced if you regularly optimize your hard disk. In this

Restore options

Choosing Options from the Settings menu and clicking the Restore tab displays a set of options for tailoring the restore operation. You can specify whether files should be restored to their original location or to an alternative location, and whether the original folder structure should be preserved or all the files should be in one folder. You can also request that restored files be checked against the backup files, and you can specify the circumstances under which existing files should be overwritten by backup files.

context, optimization entails routinely checking the integrity of your hard drive and file structure, and defragmenting the disk. We'll briefly cover both optimization procedures here.

Using ScanDisk

Contrary to what you might expect, the information in a document is not necessarily stored in one chunk but may be scattered throughout your hard disk. Your hard disk is divided into allocation units, sometimes called *clusters*, each with its own number. As you work on a document (adding information here, deleting information there, and saving as you go), Windows stores the changes to the document in the first available allocation unit and uses a sort of address book called the *file allocation table*, or *FAT*, to keep track of the units in which the parts of the document are stored.

The file allocation table

For the most part, this system works pretty well, but occasionally problems arise that can lead to loss of data. You can minimize the chances of such problems by regularly running ScanDisk to check for the following conditions:

- Bad (damaged) disk sectors

Bad sectors

- Data on the disk that doesn't have an entry in the FAT, a condition known as *lost file fragments*

Lost file fragments

- Two files that have been assigned to the same allocation unit, a condition known as *cross-linked files*

Cross-linked files

- Problems involving long filenames, your folder structure, and compressed disks (see page 107)

Filename, folder structure, and compressed disk problems

To keep your hard disk(s) in tip-top shape, you can tell ScanDisk to detect and then repair or work around any problems it finds. Here's how:

1. Click the Start button, point to Programs, point to Accessories, point to System Tools, and click ScanDisk to display the window shown on the next page.

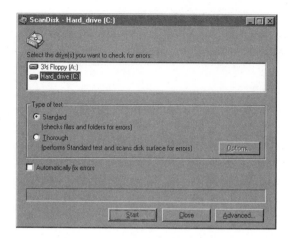

As you can see, you can use ScanDisk to fix problems on both your hard disk(s) and floppy disks, but ScanDisk can't work with CD-ROMs.

Selecting a drive

2. Be sure the C: drive is selected in the list of drives, select the Thorough option in the Type Of Test section, check that the Automatically Fix Errors option is deselected, and click Start. ScanDisk goes to work, reporting its progress in a bar at the bottom of the dialog box. (The data-area-disk-surface scan will take a few minutes.)

3. If ScanDisk finds no problems, it displays a ScanDisk Results dialog box like this one:

ScanDisk options

Clicking the Options button in the ScanDisk window displays a dialog box in which you can tailor the Thorough option. You can restrict the surface scan to a specific area of the disk, and you can restrict the test to reading sectors, instead of both reading and writing. You can also prevent ScanDisk from moving any hidden and system files that are stored in bad sectors. (Some programs may get confused if they expect to find these files in specific places.)

After reading the information in the dialog box, you can click Close to close it.

4. If ScanDisk finds a problem, it displays a dialog box to report the error with options you can select to tell it what to do. (In some dialog boxes, if you don't know how to proceed, you can click the More Info button.) Select the option you want and click OK.

If you select Automatically Fix Errors before clicking Start, ScanDisk fixes any errors it finds. How it fixes them depends on the specifications in the ScanDisk Advanced Options dialog box, which is displayed when you click the Advanced button in the bottom right corner of the ScanDisk window:

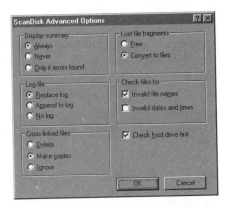

Here you can determine whether ScanDisk should display a summary of the errors it fixed and how it should handle its operations log. You can also specify the method for fixing cross-linked files and lost clusters, what file elements should be checked, and whether a host drive should be checked before a compressed drive.

Using Disk Defragmenter

Windows comes with a defragmentation program called Disk Defragmenter. Because of the way Windows stores files, your hard disk can be a checkerboard of full and empty allocation units. Disk Defragmenter uses the FAT to find all the scattered parts of each file and then stores the parts together in a contiguous group of allocation units. Working with a program or document is then easier because its file is stored in one place, and Windows doesn't have to jump all over your hard disk to put the file together.

Converting lost fragments to files

If ScanDisk finds lost file fragments, it converts each fragment to a file and then stores the file in the drive folder with the name FILE0000. (The next fragment is named FILE0001, and so on.) You can then look at the files and see whether they contain anything worth salvaging before deleting them. If all the file fragments were originally created by the same program, you might want to reinstall that program. If you can't be bothered to examine the files, you can select the Free option in the Lost File Fragments section of the dialog box that appears when you click Advanced in the Scan-Disk window. ScanDisk will then simply free up the space occupied by the file fragments on your disk.

Before running Disk Defragmenter, you should use ScanDisk as we just described to fix any FAT problems that might exist on your hard disk. A complete discussion of the defragmentation program's options is beyond the scope of this book, but here are the basic steps involved:

Starting Disk Defragmenter → 1. With no other programs open, click the Start button, point to Programs, point to Accessories, point to System Tools, and click Disk Defragmenter. You see this dialog box:

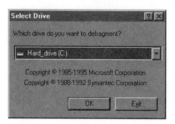

Selecting a drive → 2. With your C: drive selected in the drop-down list box, click OK. The Disk Defragmenter dialog box reports the percentage of defragmentation and a recommended course of action:

3. Click the Start button to start the defragmentation process.

4. Go and do something else for a while; otherwise, you'll find yourself staring at the graphic representation of file fragments being assembled into complete files in the program's progress window.

5. When the defragmentation process is complete, you see this message box:

Which disks can be defragmented?

Disk Defragmenter works with local hard disks and floppy disks, but not with network disks. It can handle disks that have been compressed with DriveSpace (see the facing page), but not disks that have been compressed with other compression programs.

6. Click Yes to quit the program.

If your disk was severely fragmented, you'll probably notice that operations requiring hard disk access now take less time than before.

Fitting More Information on Your Hard Disk

These days, application programs are getting bigger with each new version, and because the documents you create with these programs are likely to contain fancy formatting and perhaps even graphics, they are getting bigger, too. When you factor in the 20 megabytes of free space that Windows requires for its *swap* file (an overflow area that Windows uses when your computer's memory is full), it's not surprising if what you thought was a huge amount of storage space last year turns out to be inadequate this year.

← The Windows swap file

To tackle this problem, Windows comes with the DriveSpace program, a compression utility that enables you to squeeze more storage space out of your hard disk. If you are continually running out of space or you can't load that exciting new program because you don't have enough room, DriveSpace may be the answer.

← DriveSpace

Before you compress your hard disk, you might want to see if you can free up space by deleting programs you rarely use, by purging your folders of obsolete documents, and by purging and reducing the size of your Recycle Bin (see page 54). If that doesn't produce the additional space you need, then it's time to consider DriveSpace.

Defragmentation details

The first time you run Disk Defragmenter, you might want to click the Show Details button so that you can watch the program in action. Then you'll have a better sense of what Disk Defragmenter is up to behind the scenes.

We can't cover the DriveSpace program in detail here; our intent is to give you an idea of what's involved so that you can decide whether to take advantage of this powerful feature. Compressing a disk sounds like scary stuff, and it's certainly not for the fainthearted or the scatterbrained. For one thing, you must be diligent about backing up a compressed disk to avoid the risk of corruption and loss of data. However, the steps for creating a compressed disk are relatively simple, and the first step is to decide what you want to compress.

- If your computer has only one hard disk (drive C), you can compress that disk to gain space. (The version of DriveSpace that ships with Windows 95 can't compress disks that are much larger than 256 MB; for larger disks, you may need to compress free space only; see the tip on the facing page for more information.)

- If you have more than one hard disk, you can compress one or all of your disks.

- You can specify that no existing files are to be compressed, in which case, DriveSpace creates a new compressed drive from the free space on the designated disk.

- You can compress floppy disks.

For demonstration purposes, let's compress a floppy disk. Follow these steps:

Compressing a floppy disk

1. Insert a blank, formatted floppy disk in your floppy drive. Then, with no other programs open, click the Start button, point to Programs, point to Accessories, point to System Tools, and click DriveSpace. You then see this DriveSpace window:

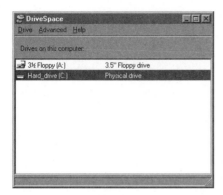

2. Select your floppy drive in the Drives On This Computer list and choose Compress from the Drive menu. DriveSpace displays this dialog box:

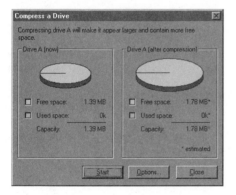

3. Click Start. DriveSpace reports its progress during the compression process.

If you compress a hard disk, DriveSpace suggests you back up your files before compressing the disk. Simply click the Back Up Files button and use Microsoft Backup to safeguard your files on disks or tape (see page 96). Then click OK to proceed with the compression operation.

DriveSpace may restart your computer while it is working its magic, so don't be alarmed if your computer seems to have a mind of its own during this process. When compression is

Compressing free space

Contrary to what you might think, compressing your free space does not shrink the amount of space you have available. It sets up your free space so that any files you store there will be compressed. You can compress the free space on a hard disk by selecting the disk drive in the DriveSpace window and choosing Create Empty from the Advanced menu. (You can't compress only the free space on a floppy disk.) In the dialog box that appears, you can usually just click Start to accept the default settings. (You might want to increase the amount of free space remaining on the uncompressed drive to allow for system files that programs you install in the future will want to add to your Windows folder.) DriveSpace then allocates most of the free space on the disk to a new drive without disturbing any existing files. The compressed drive has its own folder and shows up in My Computer and Windows Explorer just like any other drive.

complete, DriveSpace tells you how much space your newly compressed drive now has.

4. Click Close to close the Compress A Disk dialog box, and then close the DriveSpace window.

If you compress a hard disk, DriveSpace restarts your computer after is has finished the compression operation.

How DriveSpace works

So now you have a compressed disk. What does that mean? Your disk is physically the same as before; it's the files stored on the disk that are compressed, not the disk itself. With DriveSpace, compression is accomplished by using a special coding system to reduce the number of characters in each file and then cramming the compressed files together in one big master file, called a *compressed volume file* (CVF). Drive-

The compressed volume file

Space hides the CVF on an uncompressed part of the disk,

The host drive

which it designates as a new drive called the *host*. It usually assigns the host drive the letter H (unless you already have a drive H, in which case, DriveSpace uses the next available

WARNING!

letter). You should never move or mess with the CVF, because it contains all the information that was formerly stored in separate files on your hard drive.

Decompressing disks

With DriveSpace, you can decompress disks as easily as you compress them. First select the disk drive in the DriveSpace window. (If you're decompressing a floppy disk, insert the disk in your floppy drive.) Then choose Uncompress from the Drive menu. (If the Mount Drive dialog box appears, simply click Yes to mount the selected disk drive so that you can proceed with the decompression operation.) Read the information in the Uncompress A Drive dialog box and click Start. If necessary, DriveSpace then gives you the opportunity to back up any files that exist on the selected drive. Assuming that you've already backed up the compressed drive, click the Uncompress Now button and respond appropriately to any messages that appear. If you're decompressing a hard disk drive, DriveSpace restarts your computer as soon as it finishes the decompression operation.

The beauty of DriveSpace is that once you compress the disk, using programs and creating documents is no different than before, because DriveSpace does all the work behind the scenes. When you open a compressed document to work with it in a program, DriveSpace uncompresses the document in memory; when you save a document, DriveSpace compresses it and adds it to the CVF. DriveSpace keeps track of everything, including estimating how much compressed data it can add to the CVF before the hard disk will really be full.

For more information about DriveSpace, see its Help topic, which goes into more detail about the concepts we've presented here.

That's it for this chapter on problem-solving. Hopefully, being aware of the potential problems we've discussed will help you avoid them altogether and make your time at the computer more productive.

Changing Your Computer's Setup

Windows comes with a set of useful tools you can use to tailor your computer to your own way of working. We show you how to make common adjustments and briefly discuss less common ones, and then cover taskbar customization.

Relocate the taskbar on the desktop

Add new devices to your system with the Add New Hardware Wizard

Install or uninstall programs with just a few mouse clicks

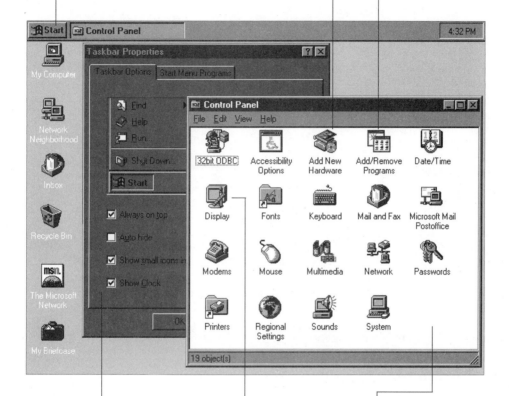

Customize the taskbar to suit your needs

Add a pattern to the desktop or activate a screen saver

Use the tools in Control Panel to tailor your computer's setup

I n this chapter, we give you a brief overview of the Windows tools you can use to change your computer's setup and add new programs. We've left this discussion until Chapter 5 because we feel you are unlikely to need these tools when you first start using Windows 95. Usually, the Windows default setup will more than meet your needs, but if you're curious, you can glance through this chapter to learn about the available options. Then when you're ready to experiment, you'll know where to start.

Most of the tools we cover in this chapter are grouped in a system folder called Control Panel. This folder is accessible via My Computer and Windows Explorer, but the easiest way to open Control Panel is as follows:

Opening Control Panel

1. Click the Start button and choose Settings from the Start menu. Windows displays a submenu containing three options: Control Panel, Printers, and Taskbar. (See page 132 for more information about Printers and page 133 for more information about Taskbar.)

2. Click Control Panel to display this window:

You can then double-click the icon representing the settings you want to change.

Adding or Removing Hardware

If you add new hardware to your computer, such as a sound card, modem, or CD-ROM drive, you will want Windows 95 to recognize this new device. With previous versions of Windows, adding new hardware could be a lengthy and often frustrating experience. However, Windows 95 features a new technology called *Plug and Play*, which makes this process easier. With Plug and Play, you still have to physically add a new hardware device to your computer, but you no longer have to fuss around with drivers and setup programs. When you turn on your computer, Windows 95 automatically recognizes the new device, takes care of setting it up, and installs any programs necessary to make the new hardware work.

◄—————————— **Plug and Play**

Sounds great, right? Unfortunately, there's a snag. To take full advantage of this technology, you must have Plug and Play support in these three areas:

- Your computer's BIOS (basic input-output system), a program built into your computer that you usually don't have to worry about

◄—————————— **Plug-and-Play requirements**

- The operating system (Windows 95)

- The hardware device you want to add

How do you know if you can Plug and Play with your computer? You are running Windows 95, so that area of support is taken care of. You know that any new hardware you buy supports Plug and Play if it has the Windows 95 logo on the box. Microsoft allows hardware manufacturers to display this logo only if the hardware has Plug and Play capability. BIOS support is the area most open to question. If you upgraded to Windows 95 without changing your computer, your BIOS probably doesn't support Plug and Play. If you recently purchased a computer with Windows 95 already installed, then it may have Plug and Play support (check the documentation that came with the computer).

For those of you with older computers, all is not lost. Windows 95 includes an Add New Hardware Wizard that makes

◄—————————— **The Add New Hardware Wizard**

Add New
Hardware

The Add New Hardware icon

adding a new device easier than it was with previous versions of Windows. When you double-click the Add New Hardware icon in the Control Panel window, the wizard displays a series of dialog boxes, asking you questions about the new device. In the second dialog box, if you select the Yes (Recommended) option and then click Next (twice), Windows searches for your new hardware and displays a list of any devices it finds. To have Windows try to determine the correct settings and install the correct driver, select the device you want to add and click Next. Then follow the wizard's instructions to complete the process.

If Windows can't locate the new device, the wizard displays a dialog box in which you can select the hardware type. You then select the make and model of the device in the next dialog box. With this help, Windows can usually install the new hardware correctly.

If the hardware you are adding is not listed in the wizard's dialog box, contact the device's manufacturer and ask for a Windows 95 driver and the instructions for installing it.

Removing hardware

If you remove a device from your computer, you'll want to tell Windows that the device is no longer available. Double-click the System icon in the Control Panel window and click the Device Manager tab to display these options:

Drivers

Each of the devices attached to your computer has an associated driver. This driver is a control program that enables Windows to work with the device. The drivers for many common hardware devices are shipped with Windows 95. If Windows doesn't recognize one of your devices, you may need to contact the device's manufacturer and ask for a Windows 95 driver.

Before we go any further, here's a word of warning: Don't play around where Windows and devices are concerned. Unless you know what you're doing, leave the settings in this dialog box alone. If you do know what you're doing, first check that the View Devices By Type option is selected and then double-click the type of hardware you want to remove to display a list of makes and models. Click the make and model of the device, click the Remove button, and then click OK.

WARNING!

Adding or Removing Programs

Setting up a program to be used under Windows 95 is not simply a matter of copying the program to your hard drive. Usually the program comes with a setup utility that makes sure all the necessary pieces are copied to the correct locations and alerts Windows 95 to its existence. If you later remove the program, not only must the program's files be deleted from your hard drive, but ideally Windows should remove all references to the program from its system files. Similarly, if you add or remove any of the programs that come with Windows, Windows 95 needs to be involved so that it can take care of the necessary housekeeping. In this section, we look at how you add and remove both new application programs and the programs that ship with Windows 95.

Adding or Removing Application Programs

To install a new application program from a floppy disk or CD-ROM, double-click the Add/Remove Programs icon in the Control Panel window to display the dialog box shown on the next page.

Add/Remove
Programs

**The Add/Remove Programs
icon**

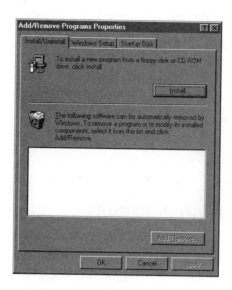

The Install Wizard ──────────►

Insert the first installation disk or the CD and click the Install button to start the Install Wizard. The wizard searches your floppy drive and CD-ROM drive for an installation program and prompts you to confirm that it should run the program. The installation program then takes over, prompting you for any information it needs.

AutoPlay

If you have a CD-ROM drive and like to play music, games, or utilize reference materials provided on a CD, you'll probably be interested in the new AutoPlay feature. AutoPlay simply means that when you insert a music CD in your CD-ROM drive, Windows assumes you want to play that CD immediately and starts the computer's CD player without you having to push play. If you load a previously installed game or reference CD in the CD-ROM drive, Windows looks for a file called AUTORUN.INF. (Only CDs that have been produced since the release of Windows 95 will contain this file.) If the file is found, Windows starts the program without any fuss.

If the application program comes with an uninstall utility, the Install Wizard adds the program to a list. If you want to remove the program, you can select it from the list at the bottom of the Install/Uninstall tab of the Add/Remove Programs Properties dialog box and then click the Add/Remove button. If the program you want to remove is not listed, look for an uninstall application in the folder where the program is stored. (It will most likely be labeled *Remove* or *Uninstall*.) If you don't find anything there, check the program's documentation or call technical support for that particular program.

Adding or Removing Windows Components

When installing Windows 95, you can choose a Typical installation or a Custom installation. Unless you chose Custom and selected all the available components, you probably don't have all the programs that come with Windows on your computer. As you work with Windows, you may find you need a Windows program that you initially chose not to install, or you may find you never use a program that you did install. With Windows 95, you can easily add or remove components at any time.

To add or remove a Windows component, double-click the Add/Remove Programs icon in the Control Panel window and then click the Windows Setup tab of the Add/Remove Programs Properties dialog box to display these options:

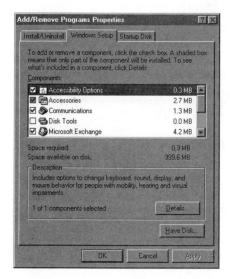

In the Components list box, Windows displays the optional components by category. Categories with all components installed display a check mark in a white box while categories with only some components installed display a check mark in a gray box. To the left of the Details button, Windows tells you how many components in the selected category are currently installed and how many are available. On the right side of the Components list, Windows displays how much hard disk space the installed components for each category use.

To add or remove a component, select the category and click the Details button. Then click the check box next to the component you want to add or remove. (Clicking an empty check box puts a ✔ in the box and adds the component; clicking a check box with a ✔ removes the ✔ and removes the component.) Click OK to close the component's dialog box,

Creating a startup disk

In the event that you ever have trouble getting your computer started, it is a good idea to create a startup disk for Windows 95. If a startup disk was not created when Windows 95 was first installed on your computer, you can create one at any time by using the Add/Remove Programs option in Control Panel. To create the disk, you will first need a blank floppy disk and your original copy of Windows 95 ready. Next, double-click Add/Remove Programs in the Control Panel window and then click the Startup Disk tab. Click the Create Disk button and follow the instructions provided. We discuss creating a startup disk further on page 92.

and then click OK again to close the Add/Remove Programs Properties dialog box.

Customizing Windows

With Windows 95, you rarely need to live with a setting that annoys you or interferes with your work. Does the color of your screen bother you? Do you wish the Start button were in a different location? Do you want to change the time displayed by the clock at the right end of the taskbar? Then this section is for you. We'll explore two categories of customization: first, the options you are most likely to want to change and can freely experiment with; and second, the options that you are unlikely to want to change and that only experienced users should mess with.

Common Adjustments

The options covered in this section are fairly easy to change, and experimenting with them can't harm your system. As you follow the instructions in our examples, bear in mind that you can actually implement a change by clicking OK in a dialog box, or you can leave the current setting as it is by clicking Cancel.

Changing the Date or Time

Date/Time

The Date/Time icon

As you have seen, the time is displayed at the right end of the taskbar, and the date is displayed in a pop-up box when you point to the time with the mouse. You can use the Date/Time icon in the Control Panel window to set your computer's date and time. Or you can right-click the time at the right end of the taskbar and choose Adjust Date/Time from the object menu. Let's try the second method:

1. Move the pointer to the clock at the right end of the taskbar and right-click it.

2. Choose Adjust Date/Time from the object menu. Windows displays the dialog box shown at the top of the facing page.

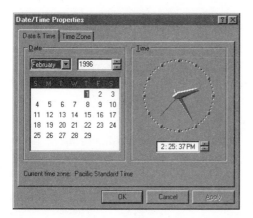

3. In the Date/Time Properties dialog box, click the arrow at the right end of the Month box and select January from the drop-down list.

4. In the Year edit box, click the spinner's up arrow until the year changes to 1998.

5. On the calendar, click Thursday, the 1st.

6. If the time needs adjustment, select the hour, minutes, seconds or AM/PM in the Time edit box and type a new entry. (You can also select each component of the time and use the spinner arrows to change it.)

7. If you want to change the time zone, click the Time Zone tab to display this map:

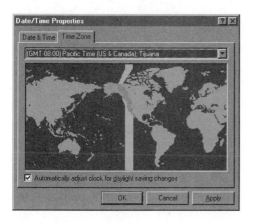

Bold object-menu commands

When you right-click an object on the Windows 95 desktop, you'll often notice that one command on the object menu appears in bold. If you had simply double-clicked the object, the bold command would have been carried out automatically. For example, when you right-click the clock, the Adjust Date/Time command, which opens the Date/Time Properties dialog box, appears in bold. If you double-click the clock instead, the Date/-Time Properties dialog box appears automatically.

8. Click the appropriate section on the map.

9. Assuming you don't really want to change the date, time, and time zone, click Cancel to close the Date/Time Properties dialog box without making any changes.

Tailoring the Display

Display

The Display icon ➤

You can adjust the look of your screen by changing its color scheme, resolution, screen saver, and other visual settings. You can access these settings by double-clicking the Display icon in the Control Panel window, but the fastest way to make adjustments to your display is to do the following:

1. Point to a blank area of the desktop and click the right mouse button.

2. Choose Properties from the object menu to open this Display Properties dialog box:

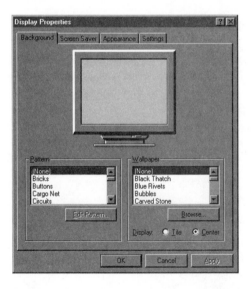

On the Background tab of the dialog box, you can easily change the pattern of your desktop. If you want something fancier, Windows comes with several bitmap graphics files that you can use to *wallpaper* the desktop, instead. (Large and colorful wallpaper files can really eat up memory, so if you're low on memory, you might want to skip the wallpaper.) Let's change the pattern of the desktop and then wallpaper it:

1. In the Pattern section of the Display Properties dialog box, click the various pattern names in the list and notice their effect on the sample screen shown above the list. When you have finished exploring, select Thatches and click OK.

Changing the background

2. Right-click an empty section of the desktop again and then choose Properties from the object menu to redisplay the Display Properties dialog box.

3. In the Wallpaper section of the Background tab, click the various wallpaper names and notice their effect on the sample screen. When you're ready, select Bubbles.

4. At the bottom of the Wallpaper section, select the Tile option to fill the entire desktop with tiled copies of the wallpaper graphic, and then click OK.

Notice that the wallpaper completely obscures the Thatches pattern you selected earlier.

If you don't like your screen's new look, you can always try a different background or return the Pattern and Wallpaper settings to (None).

In the Display Properties dialog box, you can also click the Screen Saver tab to specify whether Windows should display a moving picture or pattern during periods of inactivity. This display helps prevent static screen objects, such as window title bars and menu bars, from "burning into" the monitor. Here's how to activate a screen saver:

1. Open the Display Properties dialog box and click the Screen Saver tab to display the options shown on the next page.

Using other screen savers

After you load a screen saver program you've purchased (or downloaded from a bulletin board), you can activate the screen saver in the usual way. Just double-click the Display icon in Control Panel and select the screen saver from the drop-down list on the Screen Saver tab.

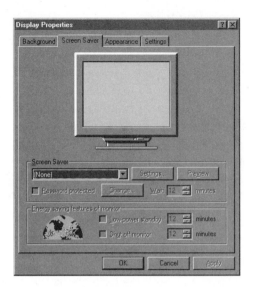

Scrolling marquees

Windows 95 provides a screen saver called Scrolling Marquee that displays text on your screen when the screen saver is activated. You can use this feature to remind yourself of an upcoming meeting or a task that needs to be completed during the day. (However, the computer must be turned on and idle for the screen saver to be activated.) To create a marquee screen saver, double-click the Display icon in Control Panel and then click the Screen Saver tab. Select Scrolling Marquee from the Screen Saver drop-down list and click the Settings button to display the settings options. Here, you can type your text in the Text edit box (for example, *Don't forget to pay the phone bill today!*) and then adjust the position and speed of the marquee and the background color of the screen. You can also click the Format Text button to change the font, size, or color of your marquee text.

2. Click the arrow at the right end of the Screen Saver box and select Flying Windows from the list of screen saver options. The sample screen shows what the screen saver looks like, but you can also click the Preview button to see its effect full-screen. (After you click the Preview button, simply moving the mouse returns you to the Display Properties dialog box.) If watching the flying windows gives you motion sickness, you can slow them down by clicking the Settings button and adjusting the speed slider.

3. In the Wait edit box, use the spinner to specify 5 minutes as the period of inactivity after which Windows should turn on the screen saver. Then click OK to apply your changes and close the dialog box.

On the Appearance tab of the Display Properties dialog box, you can change the colors of standard Windows elements, such as the scroll bars, the active title bar, and the desktop. Let's change the color scheme now by following these steps:

1. Open the Display Properties dialog box and then click the Appearance tab to display the options shown at the top of the facing page:

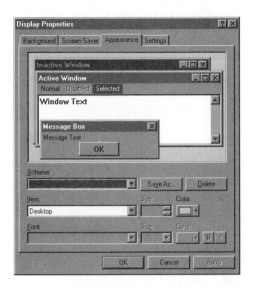

2. Click the arrow at the right end of the Scheme box and select Desert from the list of preset color schemes. Windows displays a sample of what the color scheme will look like in the window above the list.

3. To change the color of the active title bar, click the arrow at the right end of the Item box, scroll up the list, and select Active Title Bar. Then click the arrow at the right end of the Color box and select the navy-blue box (the second box in the fourth row) in the color palette.

4. While you're at it, try changing the font of the active title bar by selecting Times New Roman from the Font drop-down list. (Note that you can also change the size, color, and other attributes of the font.)

5. Click OK to implement your changes or click Cancel to ignore them and leave the current settings in place.

Playing with colors can be fun, and we encourage you to experiment with this feature to learn more about it. We also recommend that you choose colors that are easy on the eyes, especially if you use Windows a lot.

The Settings tab

On the Settings tab of the Display Properties dialog box, you can change the number of colors displayed and the *resolution* of your monitor. (Resolution is the degree of sharpness of a displayed character or image.) To adjust the color setting, simply select one of the options in the Color Palette drop-down list. To change the resolution, move the slider in the Desktop Area left or right as appropriate. If you switch to a higher resolution, you can fit more information on your screen at one time. However, if you make the resolution too high, you may have trouble reading the images on your screen. Note that depending on the type of monitor and display adapter you have, you may or may not be able to change the resolution setting.

Mouse

The Mouse icon ──────────►

Adjusting the Mouse

You can change how fast you have to double-click the mouse button or make other mouse adjustments by using the Mouse icon in the Control Panel window. Here's how:

1. In the Control Panel window, double-click the Mouse icon to display this dialog box:

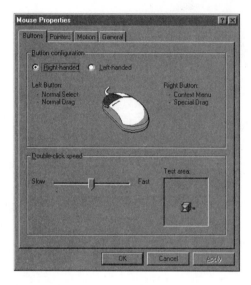

Mouse pointers

On the Pointers tab of the Mouse Properties dialog box, you can make adjustments to the size and shape of your mouse pointer. To change all the pointer shapes, select a scheme from the Scheme drop-down list. To change a specific pointer shape, first select the shape from the pointer list and click the Browse button. Then locate and select a new pointer shape in the Browse dialog box. (If you have Microsoft Plus installed on your computer, you will have even more mouse pointer shapes to choose from, such as a dinosaur, a banana, and a coffee mug.) To return to the normal pointer shapes, select (None) from the Scheme drop-down list or select a specific pointer shape and click the Use Default button.

2. On the Double-Click Speed slider on the Buttons tab, drag the indicator to the left to slow down double-clicking (in other words, to allow you to take more time between clicks and still have Windows recognize the action as a double-click).

3. Test your adjustment by double-clicking the Test Area box. The jack-in-the-box jumps up when you double-click it at the correct speed.

4. Make any necessary adjustments to the speed and click OK to close the dialog box.

You can also change the button configuration on the Buttons tab. If you are a southpaw and find it easier to click and highlight text with the right mouse button instead of the left, select the Left-Handed option in the Button Configuration section. The switch takes place as soon as you click OK.

Obviously, you would then click with the left mouse button to display an object menu.

On the Motion tab of the Mouse Properties dialog box, you can change the pointer speed and the pointer trail. By clicking the Show Pointer Trails option, you can help improve the visibility of the mouse pointer on LCD screens by creating a "trail" as the pointer moves across the screen. (It's fun to play with for a minute or two, even on regular screens.) This option takes effect immediately.

Changing pointer speed and pointer trails

Adjusting the Keyboard

If your keyboard repeats characters faster than you would like it to or if the insertion point blinks too fast or too slow, you can make adjustments in the Keyboard Properties dialog box. Let's experiment:

1. With the Control Panel window displayed on your screen, double-click the Keyboard icon to display this dialog box:

Keyboard

The Keyboard icon

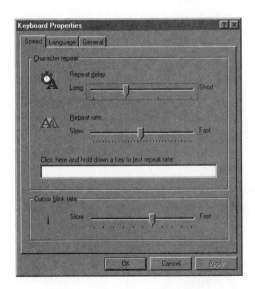

2. The Repeat Delay slider determines how long Windows waits before starting to repeat a key you are holding down. Drag the indicator all the way to the left to make the repeat delay as long as possible.

Adjusting the repeat delay

Adjusting the repeat rate →

3. The Repeat Rate slider determines how rapidly Windows repeats the key after the initial delay. Drag the indicator all the way to the left to make the repeat rate as slow as possible.

Testing keyboard settings →

4. Test your changes by clicking an insertion point in the Test edit box below the Repeat Rate slider and holding down any character key. As you'll see, Windows responds very slowly to this keyboard action.

5. Adjust the Repeat Delay and Repeat Rate sliders until you find a speed to suit your typing style.

6. If you want, change the cursor blink rate by adjusting the slider at the bottom of the dialog box.

7. Click OK to close the dialog box.

Accessibility
Options

The Accessibility Options icon →

Changing the Accessibility Options

If you have a physical condition that makes using the computer difficult, you might want to check out the Accessibility Options icon in the Control Panel window. Double-clicking this icon displays the dialog box shown here:

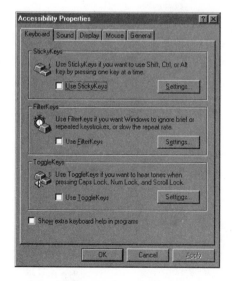

Among other options, this multi-tabbed dialog box allows you to specify the following:

- StickyKeys enables you to press the Ctrl, Alt, or Shift keys and have them remain active until you press a key other than Ctrl, Alt, or Shift. This feature is designed for people who have difficulty pressing more than one key at a time.

  Keyboard options

- FilterKeys instructs the computer to ignore accidental or repeated keystrokes. (You can also adjust the keyboard repeat rate to avoid this problem, as we did on the facing page.)

- ToggleKeys causes the computer to emit a high sound when you turn on the Caps Lock, Scroll Lock, or Num Lock key and a low sound when you turn any of these keys off.

- On the Sound tab, you can specify that visual warnings be displayed whenever your computer makes a sound, and you can tell the programs you use to display captions for any speech or sounds they make.

  Sound options

- On the Display tab, you can specify a high-contrast display and extra large type for easy reading.

  Display options

- On the Mouse tab, you can commandeer the numeric keypad to control your mouse pointer.

  Mouse options

- On the General tab, SerialKeys enables you to attach alternative devices to the computer's serial port if you cannot use a standard keyboard or mouse.

You might want to explore the various sections of this dialog box to get a feel for the many accessibility options that are available.

Uncommon Adjustments

In the previous section, we discussed adjustments you might make to the Windows environment so that your work on the computer is easier and more pleasant. In this section, we'll cover adjustments you will rarely or perhaps never make. You may want to just skim through this section, coming back to specific parts if you need to later. A word of warning: Don't tamper with the features covered in this section unless you are confident that you know what you're doing. If you have any doubts, consult someone with more computer experience before making a change.

Mail and Fax

The Mail And Fax icon

Setting Mail and Fax Options

By double-clicking the Mail And Fax icon in the Control Panel window, you can change settings for Microsoft Exchange, which handles electronic mail and faxes. Until you become more familiar with Microsoft Exchange, we suggest leaving all of the default options in place (see page 145 for more information).

Using Different Fonts

Fonts

The Fonts folder

You can use the Fonts folder in Control Panel to add screen, plotter, and TrueType fonts for use with Windows programs such as WordPad and Paint. Each font uses a small amount of memory and disk space. If you think you won't use a particular font, you can use the Fonts folder to remove it. To add or remove a font, double-click the Fonts folder in the Control Panel window to display this dialog box:

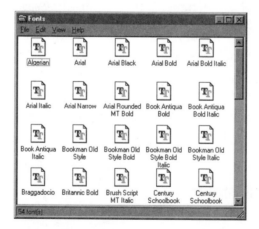

To add a font, choose Install New Font from the File menu, select the drive and location of the font, and click Install. To remove a font, right-click it in the Fonts dialog box and choose Delete from the object menu. Be careful not to delete a font that came with Windows 95, because if Windows uses that font in a menu or a dialog box, the text will disappear.

Font samples

To see a sample of a font, double-click the font's icon in the Fonts folder window. To print the sample, click the print button and then click OK in the Print dialog box.

Fine-Tuning Your Modem Configuration

You can adjust the setup of your modem by double-clicking the Modems icon in the Control Panel window. In the Modems Properties dialog box, you can add or remove a modem, change properties such as the port or the volume of the speaker, and change dialing properties. As with the mail and fax configurations, we recommend leaving the default modem configuration as it is unless you are familiar with your modem and how it operates.

Modems

The Modems icon

Setting Multimedia Options

If you have multimedia accessories on your computer, such as a CD-ROM drive, sound card, and speakers, you can make adjustments to the setup by double-clicking the Multimedia icon in the Control Panel window. In the multi-tabbed Multimedia Properties dialog box, you can alter the audio, video, MIDI (for Musical Instrument Digital Interface), CD Music, and advanced properties (depending on which accessories are installed on your computer). Most likely, you won't need to make any adjustments in this dialog box. However, if you have a multimedia computer, you might want to take a look at the available options.

Multimedia

The Multimedia icon

Configuring a Network

Unless you have general experience with computers and specific experience with your network, another icon to avoid in the Control Panel window is the Network icon. In the Network dialog box, you can change the configuration, change your computer name and workgroup affiliation, and control access to resources on your computer. Be sure to check with your network administrator before making any adjustments in this dialog box.

Network

The Network icon

Setting Passwords

If more than one person uses your computer and everyone prefers different desktop settings (such as colors and screen savers), you might have reason to use the Passwords icon in the Control Panel window. When you double-click this icon, Windows displays the Passwords Properties dialog box, where you can change your password for logging on to

Passwords

The Passwords icon

Windows. You can also click an option on the User Profiles tab of the dialog box to assign different passwords to different users so that Windows will switch desktop settings depending on who logs on to the computer.

Switching Printers

Printers

The Printers folder

If you buy a new printer, you will want to use the Printers folder in the Control Panel window to switch from your old printer to the new one (see page 142 for more information). In the Printers window, double-clicking the Add Printer icon starts the Add Printer Wizard, which takes you through the steps of adding the new printer. To delete the old printer, select its icon, choose Delete from the File menu, and click Yes to confirm your command. You can also change the settings for your printer in this dialog box, by selecting the printer's icon and choosing Properties from the File menu.

Changing Regional Settings

Regional
Settings

The Regional Settings icon

When you double-click the Regional Settings icon in Control Panel, Windows displays the Regional Settings Properties dialog box. Selecting a region from a drop-down list changes the way programs display and sort numbers, currency, times, and dates. (Changing the region doesn't affect the language used in menus and dialog boxes.)

Playing Sounds

Sounds

The Sounds icon

If you have a sound card, you can use the Sounds icon in the Control Panel window to assign sounds to system and application events. In the Name drop-down list in the Sounds Properties dialog box, you can select a sound that came with Windows (or one you have installed or created) and then link it to a specific event, such as when you exit Windows or empty

Previewing sounds

the Recycle Bin. If you want to "preview" a sound before you select it, simply click the Preview button (the small black triangle) in the Preview section of the dialog box.

Adjusting Your System

System

The System icon

Double-clicking the System icon in the Control Panel window opens the System Properties dialog box. The General tab of this dialog box gives you general information about your computer, such as what type of computer it is and how much

RAM it has. On the Device Manager, Hardware Profiles, and Performance tabs, you can change system settings that are beyond the scope of this book (though we did briefly mention the Device Manager tab on page 116). We suggest you leave this dialog box alone until you become a computer guru!

Customizing the Taskbar

As you have seen while working through the examples in this book, the Start menu and the taskbar are two of the most frequently used elements in Windows 95. Because you use them so frequently, Windows enables you to customize them for maximum convenience. For example, though the Start menu and taskbar are both located at the bottom of your screen by default, they don't have to stay there. Try this:

1. Point to the taskbar, hold down the left mouse button, and drag to the top of your screen. When you release the mouse button, the taskbar jumps to the top of the screen as shown here:

Relocating the taskbar

creen.

Maintaining data sources and drivers

Depending on your system's configuration, you may have a 32bit ODBC icon included in the Control Panel window. This icon is for database gurus who need to access databases in various formats.

4. When the pointer changes to a double-headed arrow, hold down the left mouse button and drag toward the middle of the screen to widen the taskbar as shown here:

Restoring the taskbar

5. Drag the taskbar back to the bottom of the screen. When you release the mouse button, the taskbar returns to its original size.

As well as moving the taskbar around, you can use the Taskbar Properties dialog box to change its look. Follow these steps:

Changing taskbar properties

1. Right-click the taskbar and choose Properties from the object menu to display this dialog box:

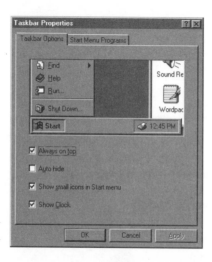

Customizing the Start menu

You can also use the Taskbar Properties dialog box to make adjustments to the Start menu. Just click the Start Menu Programs tab of the dialog box and select the desired options. For more information about customizing the Start menu, see page 63.

2. On the Taskbar Options tab, click the Always On Top option to deselect it, and notice that the window on the right in the illustration above is now over the taskbar.

3. Click the option again to turn it back on, and notice that the taskbar is now over the window. (You will probably want to leave this option selected so that the taskbar is always at hand.)

4. Click the Auto Hide option, notice that the taskbar has disappeared from the illustration, and then click OK to close the dialog box.

◄—————————— *Hiding the taskbar*

5. Point to the bottom of the screen, and the taskbar pops up. Move the pointer elsewhere, and the taskbar hides itself.

6. Display the taskbar, click the Start button, and choose Settings and then Taskbar from the Start menu to redisplay the Taskbar Properties dialog box.

7. Click the Auto Hide option to turn it off.

8. Click the Show Small Icons In Start Menu option, noticing the effect in the illustration above. Then click it again. As you can see, small icons take up less room and large icons are easier to identify. End up with whichever setting you prefer.

◄—————————— *Changing the Start menu's icons*

9. Finally, toggle the Show Clock option on and off, noticing the effect in the illustration. (You might want to turn off the clock if you have many windows open and you want to make room for their buttons.)

◄—————————— *Turning off the clock*

10. Check that all the taskbar customization options are as you want them and click OK to close the dialog box.

That concludes our quick tour of Windows 95 customization options. As we said, you will probably want to experiment with these options to discover the setup that best suits the way you work.

Communicating with Colleagues 6

We cover three ways of communicating: on paper (printing), over a network, and over phone lines. Included are brief discussions of Microsoft Exchange, Microsoft Mail, Microsoft Fax, Phone Dialer, HyperTerminal, and The Microsoft Network.

*Explore The
Microsoft Network's
multitude of resources*

*Make contact with
other computers and
bulletin boards using
HyperTerminal*

*Print your
documents and
control your
printer's setup*

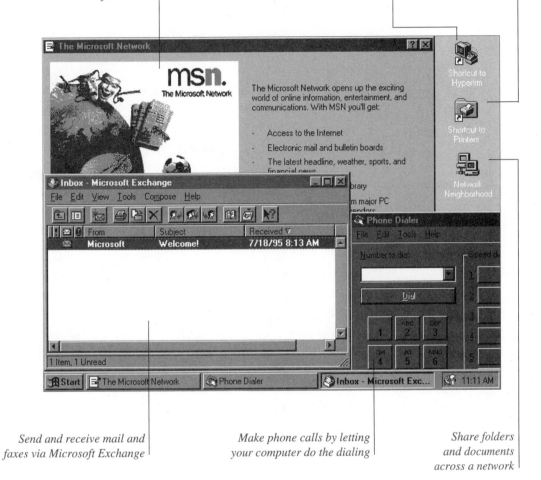

*Send and receive mail and
faxes via Microsoft Exchange*

*Make phone calls by letting
your computer do the dialing*

*Share folders
and documents
across a network*

C hapter 6 is a quick overview of three ways of communicating. First we cover how to print your documents the old-fashioned way: on paper. Then, for those of you whose computers are hooked up to a network, we look at how to communicate with other networked computers. Finally, we discuss ways that Windows 95 makes it easier to communicate with the outside world over the phone lines. Obviously, we can't hope to cover these topics in detail in one chapter. Our intention is to give you enough information here for you to start exploring on your own.

Communicating on Paper (Printing)

Although computers were supposed to usher in the era of the paperless office, in our experience they have had the opposite effect. Even with the proliferation of electronic mail (*e-mail* for short) and computer-to-computer faxes, most people still need to be able to print their documents.

With Windows 95, you have three methods for printing: using a program's Print command, dragging a document to a printer icon, and using the Send To command. Whichever method you choose, the document is printed by the default printer. If you have only one printer attached to your computer, that printer is usually the default. If you have a choice of more than one printer, the default is probably the one you use most frequently. (See page 142 for information about changing the default printer.) In this section, we assume you have installed

Local printers →

one printer that is physically connected to your computer (a *local printer*), but the procedure for printing on a printer that

Network printers →

is connected to another computer (a *network printer*) is basically the same.

Printing from a Program

You can print an open document from within a program by using the program's Print command. To demonstrate, let's print the North Directions document from WordPad:

1. Open North Directions in WordPad.

2. Choose Print from the File menu to display this dialog box, which is typical of the Print dialog box used by most Windows 95 programs:

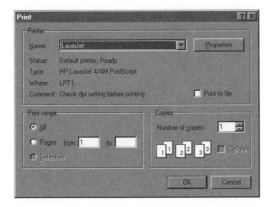

The Name box shows which printer is currently selected. The Status line tells you that this printer is the default printer and it is ready to receive your document. The Type line tells you the type of printer, and the Where line indicates the way the printer is connected to your computer. Finally, the Comment line contains any notes you have made about this printer (see page 144).

3. You want to print the entire document, so leave the Print Range option set to All. (With multipage documents, you can print only certain pages by clicking the Pages option and indicating the page numbers in the From and To boxes. Or you can select part of a document and print just that part by clicking the Selection option.)

4. Next, in the Copies section, change the Number Of Copies setting to 2.

5. Click OK to print two copies of North Directions on the default printer.

6. Close the document and WordPad.

Other printing options

The Print dialog box offers several printing options. For example, if you have more than one printer to choose from, you can use the Name drop-down list to select a printer other than the default one for a particular print job. The Status, Type, Where, and Comment lines then change to reflect the selected printer. You can get more details about the selected printer and change its settings by clicking the Properties button. (The *Printer* Properties dialog box usually includes such settings as portrait or landscape orientation and printer resolution.) Selecting the Print To File option turns the printer instructions into a file on disk instead of sending the instructions to the default location specified on the Where line. In addition to specifying the print range and the number of copies, you can tell some programs to collate multiple copies of documents with more than one page.

Dragging a Document Icon to a Printer Icon

If you need to print existing documents and you don't want to have to open them first, you can drag the documents to the icon for your printer in the Printers folder. If you often do this type of printing, you can save time by creating a shortcut to your printer on the desktop so that you don't have to open the Printers folder to print. Try this:

Opening the Printers folder

1. Click the Start button, and choose Settings and then Printers from the Start menu to open a window like this one:

As you can see, in addition to containing an icon for the Add Printer Wizard (see page 142), the Printers folder window lists all the available printers. If you have faxing capability, it is listed as well.

Creating a printer shortcut on the desktop

2. To create a shortcut to your default printer (the one that was listed at the top of the Print dialog box shown on page 139), click the printer's icon and drag it onto the desktop.

3. When Windows displays a message box asking whether you want to create a shortcut, click Yes, and then close the Printers window.

Dragging to the Printers folder

If you don't want to clutter up the desktop with a printer shortcut icon, you can drag the document icon to the printer icon in the Printers folder. Windows then starts the appropriate program, opens and prints the document, and closes the program.

4. Next, display the contents of the Directions folder and arrange the folder window so that you can see the printer's shortcut icon on the desktop.

5. Drag the South Directions document icon to the printer short-cut icon. Windows opens the document in its source program and prints the document (depending on the program, you may have to click OK in a dialog box). It then closes both the document and the program again.

6. Close the Directions window.

Using the Send To Command

If you don't want to drag documents around, you can use the Send To command on the document object menu to send files to the printer without opening them. This method works only if your SendTo folder contains a shortcut to your printer. Here's how to set up this shortcut and print a document using this method:

1. In My Computer or Windows Explorer, open the Windows folder window and then open the window for the SendTo subfolder, which looks like this:

Creating a printer shortcut in the SendTo folder

2. Click the Start button and choose Settings and then Printers from the Start menu to open the Printers folder window.

3. Arrange the Printers window so that it doesn't obscure the SendTo window. Then drag the icon for the default printer into the SendTo window and click Yes when Windows asks if you want to create a shortcut.

4. Close all the windows and then open the Directions folder window.

5. Right-click the North Directions document and choose Send To and then your printer from the object menu. (Notice that there is an entry on the submenu for each object in the SendTo window.) Windows opens the document in its source program, prints the document (you may have to click OK in a dialog box), and closes both the document and the program.

6. Close the Directions window.

Sending to other locations

When you choose the Send To command from a document's object menu, the choices on the submenu reflect all the shortcuts in the SendTo folder. These shortcuts include your floppy drive(s) and installed programs such as Microsoft Mail, Microsoft Fax, and My Briefcase.

Changing Your Printer Setup

If you buy a new printer, you can install it under Windows 95 using the Add Printer Wizard, which is available in the Printers folder. For this example, suppose you have bought an HP LaserJet 5P printer and you want to install it as a local printer. (See the tip on page 151 for information about installing and sharing or connecting to a new network printer.) Follow these steps:

Installing a new printer

1. Click the Start button and choose Settings and then Printers from the Start menu to display the Printers folder window shown earlier on page 140.

Using the Add Printer Wizard

2. Double-click Add Printer to display the Add Printer Wizard's first dialog box, click Next to display the second dialog box, and click Next to tell the wizard you want to install a local printer. You then see this dialog box:

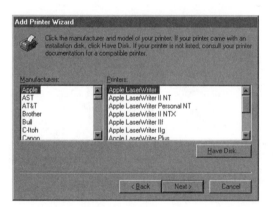

Plug and Play printers

If you buy a Plug and Play printer and your computer's BIOS is Plug and Play compatible (see page 115), Windows should recognize the printer after you connect it to your computer and be able to install it with minimum help from you. Be sure to turn off the computer when you connect the printer, and Windows will go to work as soon as you turn the computer back on.

3. Scroll the Manufacturers list on the left side of the dialog box and select HP. The Printers list on the right side of the dialog box changes to reflect the printer models manufactured by Hewlett-Packard.

4. Scroll the Printers list, select HP LaserJet 5P, and then click Next. The wizard displays the dialog box shown at the top of the facing page.

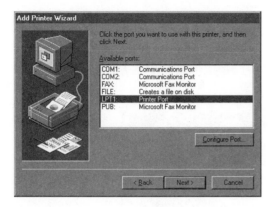

5. For purposes of this demonstration, select FILE as the port to ◀——— which the printer is connected so that you do not upset your existing printer setup. (Printing to a printer that is set to FILE sends the printing instructions to a file on a disk instead of to the printer.) Then click Next to display yet another dialog box:

Printing to a file

6. Type *New LaserJet* as the printer name, click Yes to make the new printer the default printer, and then click Next.

7. Click No to skip the test page and click Cancel if you do not actually want to install the printer. Alternatively, click Finish if you have your original Windows 95 disk(s). Windows then asks you to insert the Windows 95 disk(s) so that it can copy the driver for the HP LaserJet 5P to your hard disk. You then return to the Printers folder window, where the new printer is now listed.

Let's see the effect of installing a new default printer on your programs:

1. Start WordPad and choose Print from the File menu to display this dialog box:

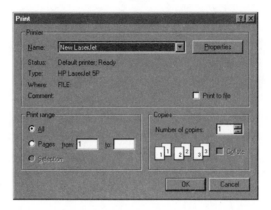

Notice that the new printer is listed in the Name box, that the Status line shows it is the default printer, and that the Where line indicates you are going to print to a file.

2. Close the dialog box and then close WordPad.

In addition to installing a new printer, you can change your printer setup in other ways. Follow these steps:

Renaming a printer

1. Display the Printers folder window if necessary, right-click New LaserJet, choose Rename from the object menu, type *File Printer*, and press Enter.

Adding comments to the Print dialog box

2. Right-click File Printer, choose Properties from the object menu, and in the Comments box on the General tab, type *Use to create files on disk*, and click OK.

Setting the default printer

3. Right-click the name of your local printer (the one that is actually connected to your computer), and choose Set As Default from the object menu to switch the default printer.

Removing a printer

4. Right-click File Printer, choose Delete from the object menu, and click Yes to confirm the deletion. If Windows asks if you want to remove files used for the printer, click Yes.

5. Close any open windows.

We'll leave you to explore printing while we move on to network communications.

Communicating over a Network

The whole point of using a network is to be able to communicate with other computers, both to send and receive messages and to share resources. In this section, we briefly cover e-mail and then discuss basic techniques for using Windows 95 to make the documents on your computer available to others and to access other people's documents.

Some of these activities may be limited by the way your system administrator has set up your network. If you see a message while following our examples telling you that you don't have this "right" or that "privilege," don't worry. The message just means that your computer is not allowed to do what you just asked it to do.

Sending and Receiving E-Mail

The Microsoft Mail e-mail (for *electronic mail*) program is shipped with Windows 95, so any network using the new operating system can use Mail for in-house communications. If your network administrator has set up Mail on your computer, you can get an idea of how it works by following the examples in this section. You will need to know the name used when Windows 95 was installed on your computer, your mailbox name, and your password to complete the steps.

With Windows 95, all e-mail and fax communications are handled by Microsoft Exchange, which provides an all-purpose Inbox from which you can send and receive messages, whether they come from a colleague down the hall or a client on the other side of the world. Follow these steps to start Microsoft Exchange and take a look at your Inbox:

Microsoft Exchange

1. Double-click the Inbox icon on the desktop to start Microsoft Exchange. Mail then displays the dialog box shown on the next page.

Inbox

The Inbox icon

Mail has entered the path for your postoffice and your mailbox name, and is waiting for you to enter your password. (If you have already logged on and selected the Remember Password option in this dialog box, Mail logs you into the service automatically and does not display this dialog box.)

2. Type your password in the Password edit box and click OK. You then see an Inbox similar to this one:

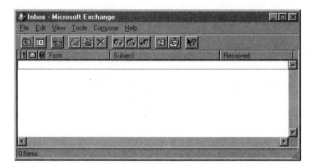

Sending Messages

With Mail, you both send and receive mail through your Inbox. We'll look at the sending side of the equation first. For this example, imagine that you are arranging the facilities for the staff's Valentine's Day party and you want to remind yourself to confirm the rental of the country club first thing tomorrow morning:

The New Message button

1. Click the New Message button on the toolbar to display a window like the one on the facing page. (If Microsoft Word is available on your computer, Exchange loads Word's New Message window so that you can use its menus and toolbars to format your message.)

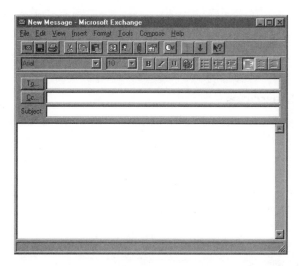

2. In the To edit box, type your name as it was entered when Windows was installed on your computer. (To send a message to someone else, enter his or her name. To send the same message to more than one person, enter their names one after the other, separated by semicolons.)

3. To send a courtesy copy of the message, you can enter the name of the recipient in the Cc edit box. For this message, leave the Cc edit box blank.

4. In the Subject edit box, type *Confirm Rental.*

5. Next, enter the message itself in the blank area at the bottom of the window. Type *Check on Deer Creek Country Club rental (555-0100). Be sure to tell them the caterers will be there at 4:00 PM to set up.* Your screen now looks like this:

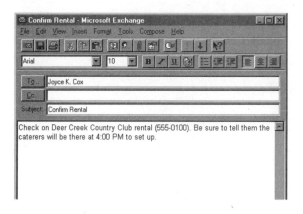

Addressing shortcuts

To help you quickly address your messages, the post office maintains a Postoffice Address List that is accessible by clicking the Address Book button in the New Message window. Click a name to select it, click the To button to transfer the name to the To box or click the Cc button to transfer it to the Cc box, and then click OK. If the Address List includes many names, type the first few letters of the desired name to scroll to that section before making your selection, or click the Find button and enter enough characters to identify the name. If you send mail only to a few of the people listed in the Postoffice Address List, you can transfer their names to your Personal Address Book by selecting each one in the Postoffice Address List, clicking Properties, clicking Personal Address Book in the Add To section, and clicking OK. You can then select Personal Address Book from the Show Names drop-down list to see the names you use most frequently. To address a group of recipients at one time, click New in the Address Book dialog box, select Personal Distribution List as the entry type, and click OK. Next, assign a name to the list, click Add/Remove Members, and add names from any of the available address books to the group. You can then select the group's name from your Personal Address Book to send the same message to all the members of the group.

The Send button

6. Send the message by clicking the Send button. Mail closes the window, and the message is on its way.

7. Minimize the Inbox window.

Receiving Messages

If you receive a message while Exchange is running, a letter icon appears in the notification area to the left of the clock on the taskbar. When you see the icon, follow these steps:

1. Double-click the letter icon to display the Inbox, which now looks like this:

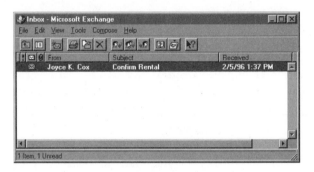

The new message is displayed in bold to indicate that you have not yet read it. The sender's name, the subject, and the date and time the message was received are all summarized, and Mail uses icons to tell you more about the message. An exclamation point means a message is urgent, and a down arrow means the message is not urgent. A paper clip indicates that a file is attached to the message.

Deciphering Mail's icons

Here's how to read the message:

2. Double-click the summary to see this message:

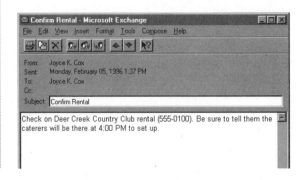

Message alert

If you can't get in the habit of checking the notification area of the taskbar, you can have Windows sound a tone on your computer, flash a different pointer, or display a message when you receive mail. In Microsoft Exchange, choose Options from the Tools menu and, on the General Tab, select one or more options in the When New Mail Arrives section.

If this message was from a colleague and required a response, you could simply click the Reply To Sender button to open a RE: window with the To and Subject edit boxes already filled in. (To send the response to the sender of the message and all recipients of courtesy copies, click the Reply To All button.) Type your reply above the copy of the original message and then send the message with a click of the Send button.

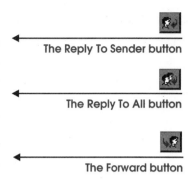

The Reply To Sender button

The Reply To All button

The Forward button

To forward the message to a colleague, first click the Forward button in the window containing the message. When the FW: window opens with a copy of the message already in the message area, enter the name of the person to whom you want to forward the message in the To edit box, and click Send.

Using Folders

When you first start Microsoft Exchange, the program creates four folders to help organize your messages: Deleted Items, Inbox, Outbox, and Sent Items. You can move messages between the folders and even create new folders by following these steps:

1. To see messages you have already sent, click the Show/Hide Folders List button on the toolbar to open a pane to the left of the message summaries pane, like this:

The Show/Hide Folders List button

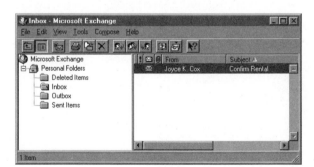

2. Click the Sent Items folder in the left pane to display the summary of your sent message in the right pane.

Displaying sent messages

3. Select the message and click the Delete button. (You can also drag the message to the Deleted Items folder in the left pane.) The message disappears from the window.

The Delete button

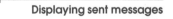

4. Click the Deleted Items folder. The message is now stored in this folder and will remain there until you select and delete it by clicking the Delete button.

To organize your mail, you can create folders for storing related messages. For example, here's how to create a new folder in which to store messages related to the staff party:

Creating folders for Mail messages

1. Click the Inbox folder in the left pane and choose New Folder from the File menu to display this dialog box:

2. In the Folder Name edit box, type *Staff Party*, and click OK.

3. In the right pane, select the *Confirm Rental* message you sent to yourself earlier and drag it to the new folder in the left pane.

We'll leave you to experiment with folders as you receive mail from your colleagues. To move on, you will probably want to minimize your Inbox so that it continues to run in the background and you can receive messages as they are sent while you are working with other programs. Or you can choose Exit or Exit And Log Off from the File menu. (Choosing Exit simply closes the program. Choosing Exit And Log Off closes the program and signs you out of Mail. Either way, your messages will be stored by the post office until you open Microsoft Exchange again.)

Quitting Microsoft Exchange

Accessing Documents over a Network

Making documents available to a network is a three-step process:

• First, your computer must be set to allow file sharing. (This option is found in the File And Print Sharing dialog box, which you access by double-clicking the Network icon in the Control Panel window. Check with your network administrator before messing with the settings in this window.)

- Second, the folder containing the documents must be *shared*.

- Third, anyone who wants to use those documents must *connect to* that folder.

In this section, we look at the second and third parts of this process.

Sharing Folders

Sharing a folder is easy, and because you can share folders rather than your entire hard disk, you can structure your folders so that only the information you want to share is accessible across the network. Moreover, you can assign passwords to shared folders to limit access to authorized people.

As a demonstration, suppose other people need to access the documents related to the staff party, which are stored on your computer. Here's how to make these documents available:

1. Using My Computer, display the My Documents folder window, which contains the Staff Party folder.

2. Select the folder that you want to share with other people (in this case, Staff Party) and choose Sharing from the File menu to display this dialog box:

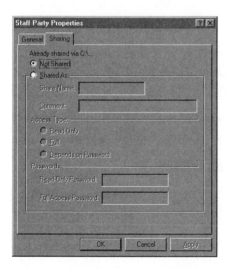

3. Click the Shared As option. The name of the selected folder appears in the Share Name edit box. If you want to give this

Using network printers

On a network, several computers can share one printer. Sharing a printer attached to your computer is much the same as sharing a drive or a folder. First, turn on sharing by double-clicking the Network icon in Control Panel, clicking File And Print Sharing, selecting the printer sharing option, and clicking OK. Then open the Printers folder, right-click your printer's icon, choose Properties from the object menu, and on the Sharing tab, click the Shared As option, type the name and any comment you want to appear in Network Neighborhood, and if necessary, type a password. Click OK to close the Properties dialog box, and then close the Printers folder. To connect to a network printer, double-click Add Printer in the Printers folder to install the driver for that printer on your computer (see page 142), designating the printer as Network, clicking the Browse button to locate the printer, and specifying if the network printer should be the default. (If a password is required to access the printer, you will have to supply it during the installation process.) You can then print documents on the network printer as easily as you can on a local printer. If other documents are being printed, your document joins a queue and must wait its turn. You can see the list of documents by double-clicking the printer icon in the notification area.

folder a different name for sharing purposes, you can enter a new name. We'll stick with the name Staff Party.

4. Click the Comment box and type any necessary identifying information. Other people will see this description in the Connect Network Drive dialog box when they are establishing connections to shared folders. As an example, type *Valentine's Day Party, 1996*.

5. Now set access rights to the folder, as follows:

- Select Read-Only to allow other people to open files in the folder but not edit, delete, or move them.

- Select Full to allow other people to edit, delete, and move files, as well as add new files to the folder.

- Select Depends On Password to allow some people full access and others read-only access, depending on the password they enter.

Setting access rights ──────────▶

For this example, select Depends On Password, and then enter the password *Valentine* in the Full Access Password edit box in the Passwords section of the dialog box. Leave the Read-Only Password edit box blank, allowing that level of access without a password. (You will give the *Valentine* password only to the people you want to have full access to the folder.)

6. Click OK to complete the sharing procedure, and when Windows asks you to confirm the passwords, type *Valentine* in the Full Access Password edit box and click OK again.

Now we'll move to another computer to show you how to access this shared folder across the network.

Connecting to Shared Folders

To use a document that is stored in a shared folder on another computer, you use Network Neighborhood to locate the folder and then, provided you have the right to access the folder, you can open its documents by double-clicking them in the usual way. Here's how you would access the files in the Staff Party folder if they were stored on another computer:

Using Net Watcher

To see who is tapping your resources, you can use the Net Watcher program, which you'll find on the System Tools submenu of Accessories, under Programs on the Start menu. (You may have to install Net Watcher first; see page 118.) When you start the program, you see a window with a list of all the computers that are currently connected to your computer and the resources they are using.

Network
Neighborhood

1. Double-click Network Neighborhood on the desktop to open the window shown here (we switched to details view):

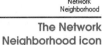

The Network Neighborhood icon

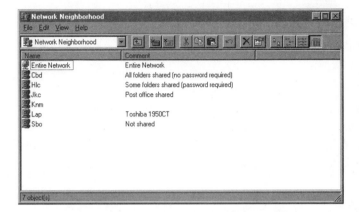

This window lists each of the computers in your workgroup and displays an icon for the Entire Network. (Clicking Entire Network shows you how your workgroup relates to others on the network and is useful when you need to share resources with other workgroups in large organizations.)

2. Double-click the computer on which the folder you want to connect to is stored. We double-clicked Hlc. Because Staff Party is the only shared folder on this computer, the window now looks like this:

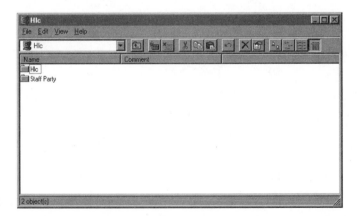

3. Double-click the shared folder to display the dialog box shown on the next page.

Useful comments

The comments displayed in the top Network Neighborhood window were entered by double-clicking the Network icon in the Control Panel window of each computer and typing a description on the Identification tab. Using comments like these can help people on large networks locate computers and documents more efficiently.

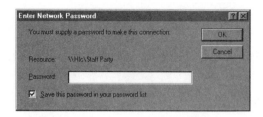

4. Type the password for the folder (in this case, *Valentine*), check that the Save This Password In Your Password List option is selected so that you won't have to enter the password again, and click OK. Windows opens the Staff Party folder and displays the Directions folder and its documents.

If all access to a shared folder requires a password and you don't know what the password is, Windows does not connect you to the folder. If full access requires a password but read-only access does not, Windows connects you to the folder and allows you to load and view files. However, you can't make changes to the documents, delete them, or move them. (You can make changes to a document and save it with a different name in a folder to which you do have access.)

To avoid having to traipse through Network Neighborhood every time you want to access this folder, you can "map" the folder to a drive letter. You can then display the drive's content in My Computer or Windows Explorer in the usual way. Here's how to map a folder to a drive letter:

1. In Network Neighborhood, click the arrow at the right end of the Go To A Different Folder box on the toolbar and select the computer on which the folder you want to map is stored (in this case, we'll select Hlc) to display the closed folder in the window.

2. Right-click the Staff Party folder and choose Map Network Drive from the object menu to display this dialog box:

Password lists

Windows creates a password list for your logon name and password to streamline the process of working with shared files and printers. When you first enter a password to connect to a shared resource, the password is entered in the password list. Then, whenever you reconnect to that shared resource, Windows uses the password from the password list instead of requiring that you enter the password each time.

By default, Windows enters the next available letter in the Drive box. For example, if you have two floppy-disk drives (A and B), two hard drives (C and D), and a CD-ROM drive (E), Windows enters the letter F in the Drive box.

3. Click the arrow at the right end of the Drive box to display a list of available drive letters, and select a letter for the shared folder. You can use any letter that isn't being used by another drive, disk, or shared folder. We'll use S (for *Staff Party*).

4. If you want Windows to attempt to reconnect to this folder each time you start the program, select the Reconnect At Logon option and then click OK. When the dialog box closes, the shared folder is selected, and its documents are listed in a new folder window, like this:

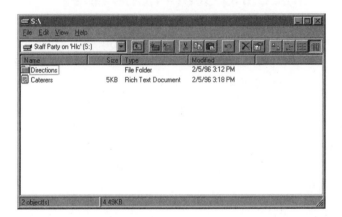

If you have entered the full-access password, you can work with the documents in the folder just as you would work with the documents on your own computer.

5. Close both the folder window and Network Neighborhood.

Stopping Sharing
If you no longer want to share a folder, you can discontinue sharing by following the steps on the next page.

Suspending sharing
If you are facing a day of crunching that will require peak performance from your computer, you can stop sharing your resources temporarily by using the Network option in the Control Panel. Choose Settings and then Control Panel from the Start menu, double-click the Network icon, click the File And Print Sharing button, and deselect the sharing options. When you close the dialog box, you will have to restart Windows so that the new setting will take effect. You can then tackle your day's work without network interference, and when the crunch is over, you can turn file and printer sharing back on again.

1. In the interests of good working relationships, warn your colleagues ahead of time that you are going to stop sharing, perhaps by sending a quick e-mail message (see page 145).

2. In My Computer, display the folder or drive containing the shared folder, select the folder, and choose Sharing from the File menu to display the dialog box shown on page 151.

3. Click the Not Shared option and then click OK.

As you have seen, Windows 95 makes using documents on networked computers as easy as using those on your own computer, hiding all the intricacies of the network so that you can focus on your work.

Communicating over Phone Lines

By combining a computer and a modem, you open up a fascinating world of communication possibilities. Although such exciting topics as the Internet are beyond the scope of this book, we'll take a quick look at Phone Dialer, Microsoft Fax, and HyperTerminal and then tell you a bit about The Microsoft Network.

Dialing Phone Numbers

At the low-tech end of modem communications is Phone Dialer, a Windows 95 program that dials any of eight stored numbers in response to a button click. It can also be used to manually dial any number. Any calls made with Phone Dialer are logged, so you could use this feature to track time spent talking to clients or to have a record of the date and time of specific calls. To use Phone Dialer, you need a modem connected to your computer and turned on, and a telephone connected to your modem. Then follow these steps:

Dial-Up Networking

You don't have to be physically connected to a network to use its resources. You can use a modem to connect to a *remote-access server* (or RAS) on the network and then access the network's resources using the Windows 95 Dial-Up Networking feature. Configuring the RAS and using Dial-Up Networking is beyond the scope of this book, but if you need more information, you can consult the appropriate Windows Help topics.

1. Click the Start button, point to Programs, point to Accessories, and click Phone Dialer to display the window shown at the top of the facing page.

2. Click the 1 button in the Speed Dial section, type *800 Numbers* in the Name edit box, type *1 (800) 555-1212* (with spaces before the open parenthesis and after the close parenthesis) in the Number To Dial edit box, and click Save. The Phone Dialer window now looks like this:

To dial the number, all you have to do is click the 800 Numbers button. You can then pick up the phone receiver and when your call is answered, talk as usual. (This is a useful number to know, but don't actually place the call unless you genuinely need a specific 800 number. We don't want to frivolously increase the workload of some poor 800 Directory Inquiries operator.)

Using speed dial

Now follow the steps on the next page to manually dial a number and check the call log.

1. In the Phone Dialer window, click the buttons corresponding to the phone number or extension of a colleague, exactly as you would push the buttons on a touchtone phone (for example, 5551212).

2. Click Dial, pick up the phone receiver, proceed with the call as usual, and then hang up.

Checking the call log → 3. Choose Show Log from the Tools menu to display this Call Log window:

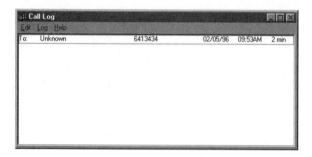

4. After checking the log, close it and then close Phone Dialer.

Sending and Receiving Faxes

Faxes have become a standard means of business communications. Although many companies still rely on a dedicated paper-based fax machine, the popularity of faxmodems means that for many people, fax capabilities are just one more communications tool built into their computers. With Microsoft Fax, the faxing program that comes with Windows 95, sending a fax is no more complex than printing a document.

To use Microsoft Fax, you need the following:

- Microsoft Exchange and Microsoft Fax must be installed on your machine (see page 118 for information about installing programs), and Microsoft Fax must be included in your Microsoft Exchange profile (see the adjacent tip).

- Your Computer must have a faxmodem or must be able to access a network faxmodem.

Exchange profiles

Before you can use Microsoft Fax, the program must be installed on your computer (see page 118) and listed in your Exchange profile. To see whether Microsoft Fax is included in this profile, double-click the Mail And Fax icon in the Control Panel window and check the list in the MS Exchange Settings Properties dialog box. If Microsoft Fax is not listed, click the Add button, select Microsoft Fax from the Available Information Services list, and click OK.

- The person you want to communicate with must have a fax machine or their computer must have a faxmodem.

- And of course, at both ends the faxing hardware must be connected to phone lines and must be turned on.

Before you send a fax, you should check your settings, as follows:

1. Double-click the Inbox icon on your desktop to display the Inbox window shown earlier on page 146. (You may have to enter a Microsoft Mail password.)

2. Choose Microsoft Fax Tools and then Options from the Tools menu to display this dialog box:

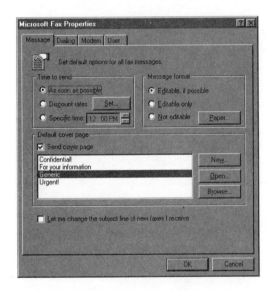

3. On the Message tab, select the Send Cover Page option and select For Your Information as the cover sheet title.

Including a cover page

4. Click the User tab and enter any information about yourself that you want to appear on the cover sheet.

5. The options on the Dialing and Modem tabs reflect information supplied when Microsoft Exchange was set up on your computer and should be correct, so click OK to return to the Inbox window.

Sending Faxes

Now let's send a fax:

Using the Compose New Fax
Wizard

1. Choose New Fax from the Compose menu to start the Compose New Fax Wizard, and click Next in the first dialog box (assuming you are dialing from your usual telephone number) to move to this dialog box:

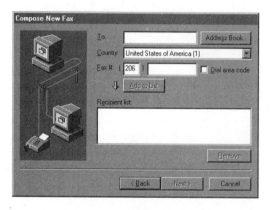

Sending the same fax to more
than one person

2. Type the name and fax number of the person you are faxing and click Next. (If you wanted to send the same fax to two people, you would click Add To List to put the first name and number in the Recipient List box, and then type the second name and number before clicking Next.)

3. Click Next to accept the default cover sheet options and display the dialog box shown here:

Adding fax addresses to the Address Book

You can add fax addresses to the Personal Address Book by clicking the Address Book button on Exchange's toolbar, clicking the New Entry button on the Address Book toolbar, selecting Fax as the type of entry, and clicking OK. Then fill out the fax recipient's information. By default, the new address is stored in your Personal Address Book, and you can select it from there the next time you send a fax to this address.

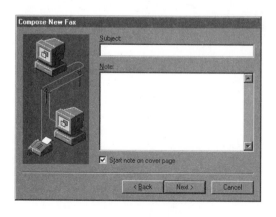

4. Type the subject of the fax in the Subject edit box and the text of your message in the Note edit box. Accept the default Start Note On Cover Page option by clicking Next.

5. Click Next to indicate that you don't want to send a document with this message. (If you wanted to send a document, you would click Add File to display the Open A File To Attach dialog box, in which you would locate the document you wanted to send.)

← Including a file

6. Click Finish. The program displays a Microsoft Fax Status box in which it details its progress as it sends the fax.

Receiving Faxes

For you to receive a fax, your modem must be turned on and Microsoft Exchange must be running with Microsoft Fax as part of its profile. (A fax machine icon in the notification area of the taskbar indicates when you can receive faxes.) An envelope icon appears in the notification area if you receive a fax, and the fax itself shows up in your Inbox and can be read just like an e-mail message (see page 148). When you read a fax sent from a faxmodem, it looks like any other e-mail message. When you read a fax sent from a fax machine, it is displayed as a "graphic" in Fax Viewer, a program included with Microsoft Fax. From there you can manipulate it in various ways to make it easier to read, and you can print it.

Connecting to Other Computers

Windows 95 comes with the HyperTerminal program, which enables you to connect your computer, via modems and phone lines, to other computers. The principal use for Hyper-Terminal is for private computer-to-computer file transfers and for connecting to local computer bulletin board systems (BBSs). Bulletin boards exist in most communities, large and small, and usually focus on specific interests. Users can post notes, exchange information, carry on computer "conversations," and so on, often for modest membership fees. (Some government agencies and corporations use free bulletin boards to provide information about their services and

Fax options

Clicking the Options button in the Compose New Fax Wizard's cover page dialog box allows you to specify the time the fax should be sent and whether the message should be sent in editable form or as an uneditable graphic image (which might be important for contracts and other legal documents). Click the Paper button if you need to specify a nonstandard size of paper or image resolution. You can also tell Microsoft Fax to use a specific cover page rather than one that is stored in your Windows directory, and you can click the Dialing and Security buttons to set retry and security options.

products.) A word of warning: Many bulletin boards carry adult-oriented materials, so we recommend that minors be supervised when using bulletin boards.

Here's how to connect to another computer or a BBS:

Connecting to another computer or bulletin board

1. Click the Start button, point to Programs, point to Accessories, and click HyperTerminal to display this folder window:

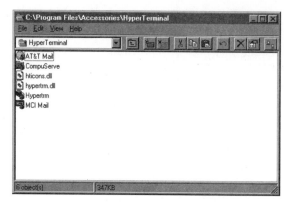

2. Double-click Hypertrm to open the HyperTerminal window and this dialog box:

3. Type a name for the computer or BBS you are connecting to in the Name edit box, scroll the Icon bar and select an appropriate icon, and click OK to display the dialog box shown at the top of the facing page.

4. Change the area code if necessary, type the phone number, and click OK to display this dialog box:

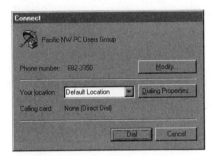

5. Click Dial to tell your modem to connect to the computer at the specified number.

6. When you want to disconnect, click the Disconnect button on the toolbar and then click the Close button. HyperTerminal asks whether you want to save this session.

The Disconnect button

7. Click Yes if you want to be able to connect to this computer or BBS again without having to reenter all the connection information, or click No to discard the information.

If you save the session, an icon for the computer or BBS is added to the folder window that appears when you choose HyperTerminal from the Start menu. You can then simply double-click the icon to open the connection and click Dial.

Quick connection

Using The Microsoft Network

The Microsoft Network (MSN) is the commercial online service that comes with Windows 95. Like other online services, such as America Online, CompuServe, and Prodigy, you access MSN by connecting your computer to the service's computer via modems and phone lines. Also like other services, you don't pay for the program that you run on your computer to access the service. But you do pay for the privilege of being connected to the service and using its resources, usually by subscribing at a flat rate for a specified number of hours a month and an hourly rate for each hour thereafter.

Unlike local BBSs, online services are at least nationwide and sometimes, like MSN, worldwide. They provide news and information on hundreds of topics and e-mail capabilities, as well as special-interest forums that often include informal online "chats." If you buy Microsoft Plus, MSN can also serve as your gateway to the Internet and the World Wide Web, giving you global researching and communicating capabilities (see the tip below).

To use MSN, you must have The Microsoft Network program installed on your computer (see page 118 to add the program if you don't have it). An icon for the service is then displayed on your desktop. The first time you double-click the icon to start the program, you are led through a sign-up procedure that includes selecting a member ID and password. Once you're a paying member, you can connect to the service, signing in with your ID and password. You then see the MSN Central window shown at the top of the facing page.

Accessing the Internet

Microsoft Plus for Windows 95 includes a program called Internet Explorer that allows you to use MSN to access the Internet. After you use the Internet Setup Wizard (located on the Internet Tools submenu) to install the program, an icon labeled The Internet appears on your desktop. Double-clicking this icon starts Internet Explorer and MSN, and after you have logged onto MSN in the usual way, you can explore to your heart's content. For example, you can click the Explore The Internet icon, click Internet Searches, and then use one of the Internet's search engines, such as Infoseek or Yahoo, to search for a word or phrase. When the results of your search are displayed, you can click on any of the blue, underlined topics and begin "surfing the net." (Remember, though, that the MSN bookkeeper is keeping track of every minute!) When you're finished, choose Exit from the File menu.

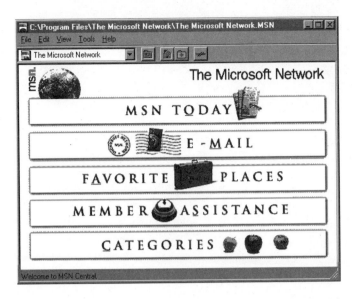

Now you can point-and-click your way around, checking out
the following:

- MSN Today for world, national, and MSN news

- E-Mail for sending and receiving messages through Microsoft Exchange

- Member Assistance for customer service

- Categories for special-interest libraries and forums

    After you've had time to explore Categories, you will prob-
    ably want to designate areas you want to visit again as
    Favorite Places. Then you can take a direct route to those
    areas in future sessions.

    When you first connect to MSN, you might want to spend a
    few moments browsing the Help topics available from the
    Help menu so that you have an idea how to move around,
    download files, participate in forums, and so on. Armed with
    this information, you'll be better able to explore. Then your
    biggest problem will be keeping track of time as you weave
    in and out of your categories of interest!

Index

Quick Course®
books—first-class training at
economy prices!

Things are looking up!

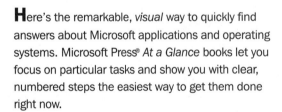

Here's the remarkable, *visual* way to quickly find answers about Microsoft applications and operating systems. Microsoft Press® *At a Glance* books let you focus on particular tasks and show you with clear, numbered steps the easiest way to get them done right now.

Microsoft Press

Get
quick,
answers—easy
anywhere!

Microsoft® Excel 97 Field Guide
Stephen L. Nelson
U.S.A. $9.95   ($12.95 Canada)
ISBN 1-57231-326-9

Microsoft® Word 97 Field Guide
Stephen L. Nelson
U.S.A. $9.95   ($12.95 Canada)
ISBN 1-57231-325-0

Microsoft® PowerPoint® 97 Field Guide
Stephen L. Nelson
U.S.A. $9.95   ($12.95 Canada)
ISBN 1-57231-327-7

Microsoft® Outlook™ 97 Field Guide
Stephen L. Nelson
U.S.A. $9.99   ($12.99 Canada)
ISBN 1-57231-383-8

Microsoft® Access 97 Field Guide
Stephen L. Nelson
U.S.A. $9.95   ($12.95 Canada)
ISBN 1-57231-328-5

Microsoft Press® Field Guides are a quick, accurate source of information about Microsoft Office 97 applications. In no time, you'll have the lay of the land, identify toolbar buttons and commands, stay safely out of danger, and have all the tools you need for survival!

Microsoft·Press

Take
productivity
in stride.

Microsoft Press® *Step by Step* books provide quick and easy self-paced training that will help you learn to use the powerful word processor, spreadsheet, database, desktop information manager, and presentation applications of Microsoft Office 97, both individually and together. Prepared by the professional trainers at Catapult, Inc., and Perspection, Inc., these books present easy-to-follow lessons with clear objectives, real-world business examples, and numerous screen shots and illustrations. Each book contains approximately eight hours of instruction. Put Microsoft's Office 97 applications to work today, *Step by Step.*

Microsoft® Excel 97 Step by Step
U.S.A. $29.95   ($39.95 Canada)
ISBN 1-57231-314-5

Microsoft® Word 97 Step by Step
U.S.A. $29.95   ($39.95 Canada)
ISBN 1-57231-313-7

Microsoft® PowerPoint® 97
 Step by Step
U.S.A. $29.95   ($39.95 Canada)
ISBN 1-57231-315-3

Microsoft® Outlook™ 97 Step by Step
U.S.A. $29.99   ($39.99 Canada)
ISBN 1-57231-382-X

Microsoft® Access 97 Step by Step
U.S.A. $29.95   ($39.95 Canada)
ISBN 1-57231-316-1

Microsoft® Office 97 Integration
 Step by Step
U.S.A. $29.95   ($39.95 Canada)
ISBN 1-57231-317-X

Microsoft Press® products are available worldwide wherever quality computer books are sold. For more information, contact your book or computer retailer, software reseller, or local Microsoft Sales Office, or visit our Web site at mspress.microsoft.com. To locate your nearest source for Microsoft Press products, or to order directly, call 1-800-MSPRESS in the U.S. (in Canada, call 1-800-268-2222).

Prices and availability dates are subject to change.

Microsoft·Press